BLS WORKING PAPERS

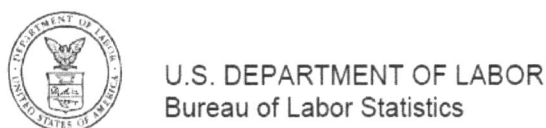 U.S. DEPARTMENT OF LABOR
Bureau of Labor Statistics

OFFICE OF PRICES AND LIVING
CONDITIONS

Using Hedonic Methods for Quality Adjustment in the CPI:
The Consumer Audio Products Component

Mary Kokoski, U.S. Bureau of Labor Statistics
Keith Waehrer, U.S. Bureau of Labor Statistics
Patricia Rozaklis, U.S. Bureau of Labor Statistics

Working Paper 344
March 2001

Using Hedonic Methods for Quality Adjustment in the CPI:

The Consumer Audio Products Component

Mary Kokoski, Keith Waehrer, and Patricia Rozaklis

Division of Price and Index Number Research
U.S. Bureau of Labor Statistics
2 Massachusetts Avenue, NE
Washington, DC 20212

Kokoski_m@bls.gov

April, 2000

Abstract

There has been a strong recommendation that the BLS explore the use of hedonic regression methods for quality adjustment in the Consumer Price Index (CPI). Until recently data limitations have made this goal difficult to implement for many categories of goods and services. This paper reports the preliminary results of employing data purchased by BLS from an outside source to produce hedonic regression-based quality-adjusted price indices for consumer audio electronics products. The effects of hedonic-based quality adjustment are examined. Hedonic indices are derived directly from the regression coefficients, and compared to the adjusted CPI values. Issues of regression specification, and practical problems for CPI quality adjustment are also addressed.

I. Introduction

There has been strong recommendation that the BLS explore the use of hedonic methods for quality adjustment in the Consumer Price Index (CPI) for decades. The Price Statistics Review Committee (the Stigler Commission Report) in 1961 expressed the view that hedonic analysis would provide a "more objective" approach to addressing quality change than the BLS standard methods of dealing with this issue (Triplett (1990)). More recently, the Advisory Commission to Study the Consumer Price Index (the Boskin Commission Report, 1996) reiterated this recommendation, recognizing that accurate measures of quality change will enable a more accurate measure of pure price, or "cost-of-living" change. Categories of goods and services where quality changes are frequent and relatively easy to identify are the best candidates for using hedonic methods, given that data can be acquired.

A price index, such as the CPI, intends to measure the effects of price changes while holding other economic factors, such as the physical attributes of the goods available, constant. In the real world, however, goods and services are always changing in their physical characteristics. This makes it necessary to find some method of subtracting out the value of quality change when the market basket and prices change. Traditionally, the BLS has used several methods of quality adjustment. These include overlap pricing, direct quality adjustment using information from producers, and linking methods. Basically, all of these methods rely upon the subjective assessment of BLS personnel (commodity analysts) in selecting newly appeared products that most closely match the disappearing ones.

Hedonic methods have been incorporated into the BLS toolkit for housing (to correct for age bias) and apparel commodities for several years. A more recent initiative in 1999 has introduced the use of hedonic methods for quality adjustment for personal computers, televisions, consumer audio equipment, VCRs, camcorders, DVD players, and even college textbooks (Fixler, Fortuna, and Lane (1999). Research is underway to evaluate these methods for refrigerators, microwave ovens, telephone services, cable television, and other goods and services. Most of these applications have required expanding the size and range of the sample of specific items in each respective category. In the CPI, the sample size for a category of good or service is a function of the relative importance of that category in the average consumer household's total annual average expenditures. For many types of goods and services where hedonic methods are likely to be useful, the sample of CPI data is too small for such an empirical application. Possible solutions to this problem are to collect additional observations on these goods for this purpose or to use supplementary data sources to provide hedonic coefficient estimates that may be used for quality adjustment when substitutions occur in the CPI sample.

For consumer audio products, the BLS is investigating the use of hedonic-based quality adjustment methods from detailed and extensive market data acquired from NPD (Intelect Group, Inc.). In this paper we present the preliminary results of this effort, examining the effects of quality adjustment on this CPI component by comparing adjusted index values to a simulated unadjusted CPI audio component. We discuss issues of regression specification, practical problems encountered in integrating results from other data sources into the CPI item structure, and also compare quality-adjusted results to a direct hedonic index from the NPD regressions themselves.

II. Hedonics and Quality Adjustment in the CPI

Quality Adjustment in the CPI:

The purpose of a consumer price index is to measure the effects of price changes on consumer households. In a true cost-of-living index, substitution behavior in response to price changes is incorporated, and the index compares two price regimes with respect to a fixed reference level of satisfaction. If a fixed weight formula, such as the Laspeyres, is used for the index, relative prices of items are compared with respect to a fixed market basket of goods and services. In either case, it is assumed that the spectrum of products, and the available attributes of the goods or services from which the consumer may choose are the same in both the reference and comparison periods.

In practice, however, the specific items on the market are often changing. Models disappear and new, different ones appear to take their shelf space. Sometimes the differences between old and new models are minor, or are regarded as such by the consumer. Sometimes qualitative changes can occur which make the new products difficult to compare to the old ones. At the extreme are goods which are sufficiently different from other items on the market as to be categorized "new goods", since they embody attributes, or specific combinations of attributes, which existing goods lack (e.g. cellular telephones, and recordable portable minidiscs). These physical changes in consumer products and services can be observed, but their value to the consumer must be excluded from a consumer price index measure. Thus, they must be identified, categorized and/or quanitified, and their implicit value to the consumer estimated.

The treatment of quality changes in the CPI has varied according to the nature and degree of the change, feasible methods for making an adjustment, and available data resources. Whether implicitly or explicitly, these adjustments attribute the observed price change between two goods as: (a) entirely to price change, (b) entirely to quality differences, or (c) partially to price change and the balance to quality difference (Kokoski (1993)). Where the observed differences between a new and disappearing product are negligible (e.g. brand of bran flake cereal), the price collector usually simply substitutes the new product for the old one. This is termed a *comparable substitution* and it implicitly attributes all of any observed price difference between the two products to pure price change. Product "downsizing", as when 16-ounce cans of tomato sauce are replaced by otherwise identical and similarly priced 14.5-ounce cans, also attributes all of the difference in price-per-ounce to pure price change (Kokoski (1993)).

When qualitative attributes between two goods are judged to be more important, then one of several methods of *noncomparable substitution* is employed. One such method, used when both the old and new product are present in at least one time period, is *overlap pricing*. In that overlap period, say period t, the price change for the item category represented by these products is given by the price change for the old product between period $t-1$ and period t. The price relative for this item category between periods $t+1$ and t is represented by the new product. Empirically seamless, this method does not require direct comparison of the prices or attributes of the two products. It implicitly attributes all of any difference in price between the old and new products to real quality difference. Where information is available on the additional cost to producers of making a specific change in the attributes of a product, then a *direct quality adjustment* may be made. This cost is then subtracted from any observed change in the price paid by the consumer for the new instead of the old product (Triplett (1988)). This direct method assumes that the perceived value of the quality change to the consumer is the same as the cost incurred by the manufacturer to provide it.

In the absence of either overlapping prices or independent information from producers on the costs of qualitative changes, a *linking method* is employed to make noncomparable substitutions. Aside from sample rotations, when entirely new and independent product samples are drawn for the CPI, linking techniques are the most prevalently used in the CPI (Armknecht and Weyback (1989), Fixler (1993)). In this case the old product makes its final appearance in period $t-1$ and the new product, which effectively replaces it on the retail shelf, first appears in period t. Since the two products cannot be directly compared in the same time period, the price change between period $t-1$ and period t for this good is proxied by the observed price change between these two periods by other goods in the same goods category. The new product then represents the good in the price index for subsequent time periods. This method assumes that pure price changes are likely to be the same for all goods in a class (e.g. price changes for cotton Oxford shirts will be the same as for other types of shirt). By implicitly imputing a price to the new product in period $t-1$, had it existed then, this method attributes some of the price difference between the new and old products to pure price change and the rest to quality differences between the two products (Kokoski (1993)). All of the above methods would miss any pure price change imposed by the producer at the opportunity offered by model changeovers.

In all these cases, some degree of judgment by the BLS commodity analyst is required. For comparable substitutions, the analyst selects the new item which most closely resembles the old one and judges any differences between them to be negligible. For noncomparable substitution methods, the new item is still chosen on the basis of this criterion, and then quantitative adjustments applied as the new item enters the index.

The currently preferred method of quality adjustment is the *hedonic method*. This method (or class of methods (Triplett (1990)), relies on statistical techniques to estimate the implicit prices of product characteristics from observed prices and quantities sold in the marketplace. These implicit prices may then be used as measures of the value of observable qualitative differences in products to consumers, and thus help disaggregate the observed price difference between two products into quality change and pure price change. The first application of hedonic methods to the CPI was in the apparel categories (Armknecht (1984), Armknecht and Weyback (1989)). Initially, hedonic regressions were estimated on the CPI sample, and the coefficient values for the attributes used to provide a structured set of criteria for selecting the most comparable substitute for a disappearing item. For example, if the fiber content of a jacket was statistically significant and a quantitatively substantial attribute in determining the jacket's price, then the new jacket chosen for the CPI sample would have to have the same fiber content as the old one. This procedure then advanced to using the hedonic regressions to provide estimates of quality change directly into the index (Liegey (1993), Armknecht, Moulton, and Stewart (1995)). For example, when a new jacket was brought into the index to substitute for a disappeared one, its introductory price was quantitatively adjusted based on the coefficients from the hedonic regression on that apparel category. The use of hedonic regressions in apparel employed the data collected by BLS for the CPI, and was facilitated by a fairly large sample, and relatively easily identified and empirically manipulated characteristics information from the CPI checklists.

Hedonic methods are now used for other categories of goods and services in the CPI. These include personal computers, televisions, consumer audio equipment, VCRs, camcorders, DVD players, and even college textbooks. Proposals to do the same are currently being evaluated for refrigerators, microwave ovens, washers and dryers, telephone services, and cable television. In some cases, a larger number of price quotes is being collected to expand the sample and thus provide a sufficiently large database for estimating hedonic regressions. Because expanding sample size is not a costless endeavor, in other cases the BLS has acquired information from data sources outside the agency for this task. These include data purchased from A.C. Nielsen, collected from electronic scanners in retail outlets, data gleaned from published sources such as *Consumer's Digest* (Liegey and Shepler (1998)), and data purchased from independent firms which collect and process retail transactions information. For consumer audio products, data are being purchased from NPD. While large and detailed, these other data resources do present some additional issues for quality adjustment of the CPI: (a) the samples are not collected under the same probability sampling procedures used for the CPI sample, so the relative degree of representation of specific models in the respective samples will differ, (b) the item definitions, categorization, and attributes identified will differ, and c) the representative outlets from which the BLS collects price quotes for the CPI differs from those sampled by other data sources, thus effecting the product mix and prices.

Hedonic Methods for Quality Adjustment:

The concept of empirical hedonic analysis can be traced to the 1930s (Court (1939)), and its application to price indices to a major work by Griliches (1961). Since then theoretical foundations have been established, and debated, for the methodology and its interpretation in economics. The theoretical basis is attributed to Rosen (1974), whose model describes a market equilibrium in which consumers select goods on the basis of the characteristics they embody, and implicit prices for these characteristics emerge which represent the value placed on them by consumers. These implicit prices represent equilibrium prices in characteristics space, tangency points between production isoquants and consumer indifference curves in "implicit markets" for characteristics. A large literature exists on the interpretation and empirical applications of hedonics, and a useful summary of the basic concepts and issues are available in Triplett (1986), (1988), (1990)).

At the most general level, the hedonic function describes the relationship between the observed market prices of physically heterogeneous goods and the amount of various characteristics which these goods embody. The *hedonic hypothesis* states that "heterogeneous goods are aggregations of characteristics, and economic behavior relates to the characteristics" (Triplett (1988), p. 630). For consumer price index applications, it is the consumer side of the behavioral equation which is of most interest. It is assumed that the consumer optimizes his consumption of characteristics by choosing the good which is closest to his or her optimal bundle of characteristics, given his or her budget constraint and the implicit prices of those characteristics. The implications of this behavior depend on more explicit assumptions of the nature of the relationship between goods and characteristics: there may or may not be a continuous spectrum of goods varieties embodying various levels of various characteristics; characteristics may or may not be amenable to "repackaging" by the consumer (analogous to the separability problem in goods space) (Fisher and Shell (1972)); and, the information supplied by the model does not necessarily inform about the function and parameters of the demand function.

Nonetheless, there appears to be a consensus that empirical hedonic analysis does provide meaningful information for inferring the value consumers place on quality changes, and the estimates from hedonic regressions can be reliably used to make quality adjustments to price indices (Triplett (1988), (1990)). This may be done in one of several ways. First, one can identify a disappearing product and select a substitute, then make a quality adjustment to the observed price of one or the other item to make them statistically comparable in quality. These are "indirect methods". In one such method, one would multiply the hedonically-derived implicit price of a characteristic by the difference n the level of that characteristic between the old and new product. One then subtracts this quality change value from any observed price difference between the two products. Another such method is to impute the price of an item in a period before it appeared on the market, using the hedonic coefficients and the observed characteristics of the product at issue. This imputes a reservation price for the newly appeared good. Alternatively, one could adopt a "direct method". Under this approach one estimates a quality adjusted price index directly from the hedonic regression itself. Along with the characteristics variables, one specifies time period dummy variables in the hedonic regression; the coefficients on these time dummies are then interpreted as the price differences between the specified period and the reference period net of changes in the quality attributes of the goods available in each period (Triplett (1986). If the relative weights of each characteristic, or the models embodying them, remain the same, then these methods should, in principle, yield similar results. In practice, since the direct method relies upon samples from different time periods, it is unclear how the characteristics' implicit values, and therefore the regression coefficients, may change over time as the overall product market evolves.

Whichever method of hedonic quality adjustment is applied, there are several empirical issues to be addressed. The issue most familiar in the hedonic literature is that of choosing an appropriate functional form. Theory does not provide guidance on this issue and much debate has been waged on it in the empirical context. Although other forms cannot be ruled out *a priori* (see, for example, Arguea and Hsiao (1993)), the most empirically convenient has not been demonstrated inferior in most applications, either. This is the semi-logarithmic form, where the log of the good's price is regressed on a linear specification of the characteristics, and time dummies where desired (Griliches (1971), Triplett (1987)).

In the context of quality adjustment of intertemporal price indices, the stability of the hedonic regression coefficients over time is an important concern. Hedonic regressions are often estimated on a cross-section sample, and thus capture a snapshot of the market at a point in time. As the varieties of goods available, and other factors change, the relationship between the goods' characteristics and their implicit prices may change (i.e. shifting demand and supply curves in the implicit characteristics markets). Thus, the hedonic coefficients from one empirical study may not provide reliable quality adjustments for the index in future periods. Even in regression equations which include time dummies, it may not be reasonable to assume that the coefficients on the characteristics variables are constant over the whole sample. Edmonds (1985) found in his study on housing that his hedonic model was stable, but this observation cannot be generalized. Silver (1998) has identified as a potential source of price index bias changes in the pricing strategies for existing models by companies as they begin to market new ones. This effect could also be reflected in characteristics space, as companies change the implicit prices offered for various attributes of the goods (for example, wireless headphones might begin to replace the wired ones which are bundled in models of portable stereos). If hedonic methods are used to adjust a price index, it is prudent to estimate the model again periodically, and attempt an analysis of the conditions under which the model coefficients change, and are thus likely to change in the future.

Other empirical issues relate to the quality and quantity of data available for performing the hedonic analysis. Errors in measurement of characteristics variables can be important (Epple (1987)). Especially in cases where data are acquired from other firms or agencies, it is important to assess how these data are collected and the nature of any averaging or imputation applied to them before using them to specify hedonic regressions to be applied to independent samples such as the BLS data. It is important that economically relevant characteristics information be provided by the data, so that the regression specification is meaningful. Another important consideration is that these data represent transactions, not list prices, since the former are the market prices which reflect consumers' preferences through their demand behavior. It is also likely that for many durable goods categories, such as electronics products, few consumers pay full list price and the relationship between list price and the average market retail price is unknown. Another concern is the potential for selection bias in the outlet or product sample, which may result from the methods used to collect the data (e.g. only outlets which use electronic scanners) or package it (e.g. elimination of outliers, imputation of missing values, substitutions among items).

III. Application to the Consumer Audio Products Sector

<u>The Consumer Audio Products Market:</u>

Consumer audio products comprise heterogeneous categories of durable goods. These range from home stereo receivers, amplifiers, and loudspeakers to pocket-sized headphone radio/cassette players. Individual products range in price from thousands of dollars to less than twenty dollars. Because most consumer audio products are physically durable for decades, technological obsolescence is the main reason for the consumer to replace or add to his or her stock of these goods. Product innovations range from making portable radios smaller and increasing the number of compact discs that can be accommodated by a CD player to major upgrades such as the replacement of turntables by compact disc players. In many respects, this class of products is not unlike personal computer goods. As with computer hardware, the specifications which describe quality changes are usually easy to identify and quantify (e.g. watts per channel, frequency range, size), and there are many brands, models, and varieties of features on the market. These quantifiable aspects of the consumer audio product category facilitate hedonic analysis.

The merging of video products and computers with audio products is occurring, as evidenced by the market proliferation of home theatre systems, magnetically shielded computer speakers, Internet radio, and compression algorithms which permit music and voice to be downloaded digitally from the Internet. The Consumer Electronics Manufacturers Association reports that consumers are seeking to complement their home theater systems with high performance audio goods. [1] As household penetration of home theater systems increases, demand for high performance audio goods will rise, effecting product quality and prices in the overall audio product market.

The consumer audio products market is an interesting candidate for hedonic analysis also because of technological innovations that have recently occurred, but have yet to penetrate the U.S. market. The MiniDisc, originally introduced as a digital replacement for the analog cassette, offers the portability of a headphone cassette player, the sound quality of a CD player (with less skipping), and the ability to make custom digital recordings directly from CDs. At present, consumer satisfaction with analog cassettes and the prevalence of CDs has left U.S. consumers disinterested in the new format. As digital products gain consumer acceptance and more prerecorded music becomes available on MiniDisc, consumer demand is likely to increase. As electronic products become digital, more of these once distinct and separate products can begin to interact and communicate with each other.

MiniDisc represents a new good, but one which combines attractive attributes of several goods familiar to the consumer. These changes provide an opportunity to examine the implications of new goods as they begin to affect the market. Is it possible, for example, to predict the market price of a MiniDisc unit, based on the hedonic coefficients of its attributes as embodied in other established products and other empirical information?

The audio products market is summarized in Figure 1, which shows the number of units sold by product category from February 1997 through March 1999based on the NPD data (described in the next section). Figure 2 shows the relative proportion of consumption devoted to each audio product category, averaged over the February 1997 through March 1999 period. Portable CD Players and headset stereos, part of the portable audio market, are the largest selling items. Figure 2 suggests that shelf systems, which are similar to but smaller than rack systems, are rising at the latter's expense. This finding confirms claims by the Consumer Electronics Manufacturers Association that consumers are moving towards sleeker compact systems and away from large rack systems. Figure 3 shows the average vintage

---

[1] Consumer Electronics Manufacturers Association, 1996. "Consumers Looking to Enhance Home Theater with High Performance Audio."

of specific items in each category, or the average number of years that a specific make and model is extant in the market, as of March 1999. These vintages do not vary much by category.

The Data:

The data used in the hedonic regression analysis were purchased by the Bureau of Labor Statistics from NPD, a private firm which specializes in the collection and packaging of such market data for sale. These data were generated from point-of-sale observations in various retail chain outlets and each observation represents the average price for a specific product model over a bimonthly (before January 1998) or monthly (after January 1998) period for each of several classifications of retail outlet types called "channels."

The NPD data consist of thirteen categories of products: CD players, portable radios, solid state recorders, portable tape recorders, portable radio cassette players, stereo headset, stereo headphones, receivers/amplifiers/tuners, cassette decks, home speakers, one brand rack systems, and shelf systems. The channels represented in the data include department stores, mass merchandisers, electronics specialty stores, and catalogue showrooms. Each observation consists not only of an average price, but also includes information on the physical attributes of each model and number of units sold. The BLS has been purchasing these data since the February/March bimonthly installment in 1997, and, for each such installment performing a preliminary analysis to check for errors or inconsistencies, and correcting them where necessary. For the purposes of empirical analysis over all these data installments, the monthly data were averaged to create bimonthly periods of data for years 1998 through January 2000.

The price and quantity observations supplied by NPD are national estimates. NPD receives data from a subset of all the outlets that sell consumer audio electronics products. The unit sales reported by these chains are then extrapolated to reflect national aggregate sales and expenditures. The extrapolation process is straightforward. First, the chains within the sample are categorized into channels. Then, the chains within each channel are assigned to cells depending on their total revenue and the number of stores in the chain. Each chain is then assigned an adjustment factor corresponding to the number of chains with similar size characteristics, nationally divided by the number of chains with similar characteristics in the NPD sample. This adjustment factor is used as a weight when aggregating chain level data on units sold and total expenditures. The average price reported for each model is then calculated by dividing total expenditures on that model by the total number of units of that model sold.

Although these data do not consist of individual retail transactions, they do represent a much larger number of transactions and models of products than the BLS data. They also include detailed characteristics information, as well as information on the first date when each particular model appeared in the NPD sample. If the inaugural date of appearance of a model is known, then these data could potentially provide quantitative information that would help track price change over the life cycle of a model. Vintage information is useful in ascertaining the introduction and proliferation of new technologies in the audio products market.

Audio product data collected by the Bureau of Labor Statistics are classified in an item stratum called "Audio Equipment: RA05." For each monthly index, approximately 167 price quotes are used to construct the price index for item stratum RA05. Data are further broken down into car audio equipment and non-car audio equipment. A CPI checklist for the audio equipment item stratum is included as Appendix Figure 1. Attribute data collected by the BLS are somewhat limited in scope and do not capture important product characteristics such as product introduction date, buffer memory, and recent technological advancements such as surround sound capabilities. Several variables that appear on the checklist are difficult to use in the context of hedonic regression analysis. These factors, as well as small sample size, prevented the use of CPI data in hedonic regressions. Therefore, we used the NPD sample to obtain coefficient estimates to quality adjust goods in the CPI sample.

Model Specification:

For the hedonic regressions, we estimate models of the log-linear form.

$$\ln p_i = \gamma' x_i + \beta' t_i + \varepsilon_i,$$

i indexes observations, p_i is the price of observation i, and x_i and t_i are the vectors of characteristics and period dummy variables associated with observation i. Finally, ε_i is taken to be the effect of unobservables on log price, which are assumed to be independent of x_i and t_i. This model was estimated separately for the thirteen categories of audio commodities defined by the NPD data, with the vector of attributes specific to each category. We model the characteristics that are continuous or near continuous nonlinearly by allowing them to have quadratic and sometimes cubic effects on log price. Categorical characteristics are modeled using dummy variables.

While the characteristics variables include many of the important attributes of a given product, there are additional attributes that are unobserved but may also affect a consumer's valuation of the product. For instance, while we can control for whether or not a portable CD player has a memory buffer, we have no information concerning the player's size and weight. It is possible that newer models may have more valuable unobserved features. We attempt to control for these by including a variable for the vintage of a given model. The vintage variable is calculated as the difference in years between March 1999, and the year and month that the model first appeared in NPD's survey. Hence, the lower the vintage the newer the product. To the extent that newer models have unobserved but valuable features, inclusion of the vintage variable in the vector of characteristics x_i will help to control for these quality changes.

While it is conjectured that vintage helps to control for unobserved characteristics, there is also the possibility that it is picking up some of the price change that would otherwise be subsumed by the time period dummy variables. If manufacturers and/or retailers use the introduction of a new model to adjust their pricing on a given set of characteristics, then it is likely that the coefficient on vintage will reflect some of those price changes. Thus, it could be debated whether or not the vintage should be included in the hedonic regressions. To examine its effect on the model, the regression is estimated with and without this dubious variable and the results compared.

To use these empirical results to quality adjust the simulated CPI, we first observe those cases where a substitution has been made in the CPI sample. Where one product model has replaced another in the CPI sample, we add to the old product's price a value equal to the coefficients on those quality attributes which differ between the two. Thus, if the old product was an Aiwa with the same measured physical attributes as the new Sony which replaces it, we add to the old product's price the difference in coefficient values between Sony and Aiwa brands.

The interpretation of the coefficients on the period dummy variables is often described somewhat vaguely as a hedonic price index. They therefore provide direct hedonic price indices from the NPD data, which can be compared to the results of quality adjusting the (simulated) CPI for these goods. There are, obviously, differences in the two samples that would cause the results from the two approaches to differ. In the NPD, the data are from independent samples in multiple periods, rather than the CPI approach of tracking price changes for an individual product on a specific outlet shelf. Not every product is priced in every period in the NPD, and regression-based methods where a coefficient on the time period dummy variable is being calculated do not require that the same good be observed in the periods being compared. Therefore, regression or hedonic indices differ from standard price indices not only in the fact that they can control for quality changes in goods over time, but also in the fact that it is not necessary to exclude goods from the calculation that appear only in the first or last period. To construct an hedonic index with similar sample characteristics as the CPI, we estimate the hedonic regressions also on a subset of the NPD data, the subset consisting of those product models present in all time periods under study. These are "restricted sample" models. Unfortunately, while it would have been interesting to compare direct hedonic index results from regressions on both the NPD and CPI samples, the CPI sample sizes proved too small for this empirical procedure.

We also estimate hedonic indices using both unweighted least-squares and weighted least-squares. For the weighted case, we use a good's average expenditure share over all periods for which we observe sales as the weight for that good in every period that it appears in the data. The hedonic indices calculated using this weighting scheme are meant to be comparable to the Tornqvist, which is the geometric mean of price relatives with average expenditure shares as weights.

Analysis and Results:

Tables 1-6 contain the results from the hedonic regressions for table CD players, portable CD players, main stereo speakers, surround speakers, [2] receivers, and shelf systems. Aside from the characteristics variables listed on the tables, the regressions also include dummy variables for manufacturer. Since this is an extensive list, the coefficients on these brand name dummy variables are included in a separate table in the Appendix (Table A.1). As is described in the previous section, the regressions are estimated using unweighted and weighted least-squares methods, and also with the vintage variable included and excluded. The time dummy variables are bimonthly because the earlier installments of the NPD data were provided on this basis.

These model specifications restrict the coefficients on the characteristics variables to be time invariant. To test the acceptability of this hypothesis, we also estimated these models for the unrestricted case where all of the characteristics were allowed to have a different effect in each time period. We tested the validity of the assumed restriction,[3] and found that, with a single exception, the hypothesis could not be rejected. The single exception occurs in the weighted least-squares regressions for shelf systems, the category which seems to be expanding most rapidly in sales volume among the audio products. If the coefficients on characteristics are allowed to change over time, then the coefficients on the time dummy variables only reflect the inflationary price effects on models with the reference characteristics and the interpretation of hedonic-based indices would be suspect. Thus the acceptance of time-invariance, generally, is reassuring for our study.

In most cases the coefficient estimates reported in Tables 1-6 have the expected sign. There are a few notable exceptions, however. For instance, in the case of receivers, the presence of a Dolby prologic decoder has a statistically significant negative effect on price, compared to the reference of no surround sound decoder, in the unweighted regressions. This superficially unexpected result may follow from the observation that some very high-end low-sales-volume models do not have surround sound decoders, while most mid-level higher sales-volume models do. In the unweighted regression these high-end

---

[2] NPD reports main stereo speakers and surround speakers in the same category. We split the category because many of the characteristics applied only to surround speakers and, hence, it did not seem appropriate to estimate these two types of speakers in the same regression.
[3] The results from these regressions are not reported in the paper.

receivers have a larger impact on the overall coefficient estimates. This may thus represent an example of characteristics bundling, where particular attributes are found only on products with other specific attributes. The prologic decoder may be providing a proxy for middle-range quality products.

The coefficient estimates from these NPD regressions were then applied to make quantitative quality adjustments to those cases in the CPI sample where one product was substituted for another. Because the CPI is a Laspeyres index, and because vintage information is unavailable for CPI sample items, the unweighted, vintage-excluded regression model was used to supply the coefficient values. To arrive at the quality adjustment factor, the differences in the exponentiated values of the coefficients for the relevant dummy variables were added to the differences in the coefficient values for continuous variables. For example, consider the case where the discontinued product is a Pioneer 100-watt-per-channel receiver, with an observed price of $179.99 in its last period of inclusion in the CPI. Its chosen replacement in the CPI sample was a Sony 500-watts-per-channel receiver, so that the quality-adjusted price is $214.57. The reliability of the procedure depends on the degree to which the most relevant attributes are captured empirically by the regressions and can also be identified for the products in the CPI sample. In most cases, however, the price predicted by the regression model was a very reasonable estimate of the observed price of the actual new product on its inaugural period in the CPI sample (sometimes within a dollar or two). The only variable which could not be used explicitly in the quality adjustment assessments was vintage, but, for those few cases where the CPI model number matched the NPD model number (so we could be sure they were identical products) we found that the vintage of the model chosen by the CPI staff as a substitute was very close to that of its disappearing counterpart. Thus, although perhaps not consciously, the CPI field representatives are selecting substitutes of similar physical character by selecting those of a similar vintage.

The results of the quality adjustment are provided in Table 7. The first column reports the replicated CPI for audio components as a combined category, as simulated by an algorithm developed by the BLS to replicate the published CPI as closely as possible. Its month-to-month changes are also reported, in the second column. The third column provides the replicated CPI with the regression-derived hedonic quality adjustments included, and its corresponding month-to-month changes. Interestingly, the quality adjusted index values do not decrease as rapidly as the unadjusted ones. A similar pattern was found by Liegey and Shepler (1999) for videocassette recorders (VCRs) in the CPI. This is a small sample, with relatively few substitutions occurring, and the statistical significance of the index values is unknown. However, as for VCRs but unlike cars and computers, there is no model-year turnover pattern to audio products marketing. Innovations do not rapidly supplant existing models, obsolescence is seldom a factor (at least for the time period of our study. Also, the products chosen as substitutes are of similar vintage to the disappearing ones, not the newest models on the market, so that the average vintage of the

CPI sample is probably older than that of the current market as represented by the NPD data. Thus, quality adjusting the audio products component of the CPI would not be expected to result in a more rapidly decreasing index.

As a benchmark for comparison, indices for the NPD-defined product categories were calculated from the NPD data itself. These are reported in Table 8. The first five rows of the table provide the standard indices for the bimonthly periods from February/March 1997 to December1999/January 2000. These are calculated by matching average price observations over time for the NPD models. As required by the index formulas, we only include models in the calculation for which prices are reported in the reference and comparison periods. Since we wish to compare these indices also to the hedonic indices from the regressions, we have dropped observations from the NPD sample with incomplete characteristics information. Because we have several time periods available for analysis, we calculated not only the Laspeyres index, but also the Paasche, Fisher, geometric mean, and Tornqvist formulas. These are all reported in the first set of rows of the table. By mathematical necessity, the geometric mean values are uniformly less than the Laspeyres, and, as expected, the Fisher falls between the Laspeyres and the Paasche index values. Unexpectedly, however, the Laspeyres index is below the corresponding Paasche index for all but one category of products. When price changes result only from changes in the supply side of the market one would expect the substitution effects to result in the Laspeyres being lower than the Paasche. That is not likely occurring in these data, but all of these categories do show a substantial price decrease over a relatively short period. The Laspeyres indices for portable CD players, receivers, and shelf systems indicate a decrease in price of more than forty percent.

The next four rows of Table 8 report ordinary least-squares regression-based indices for different samples and with the vintage variable included and excluded. The index value is calculated as the exponentiated value of the estimated coefficient on the dummy variable for the final period, times 100. The hedonic indices are calculated from the results presented in Tables 1-6. In the restricted sample regression index, the coefficient on the final time period dummy variable was estimated with no other covariates and the same set of prices that were used in the calculation of the standard indices. Therefore, the restricted sample regression includes no prices from periods other than the first and last or from models without a price in either the first or last periods. Hence, any difference between the restricted sample regression indices and the standard indices is solely a result of the fact that the formula for the regression-based index differs from that of the standard indices.[4]

As with the standard price indices, the restricted sample only considers the price effects of models in existence in the first and last periods; new models are considered noncomparable to any models

---

[4] The unweighted restricted sample regression index is mathematically identical to an unweighted geometric mean index. This fact can be easily verified using Equation (1).

dropping out of the sample. Therefore, these indices will miss changes in price associated with the introduction of a new model. For instance, a new higher quality model might be introduced at a similar price as an older model and, hence, should be registered as a (quality-adjusted) price decrease. On the other hand, the introduction of a new model might be considered an opportunity to raise prices and hence, represents a pure price increase. In Table 8, the regression index calculates a price index from the coefficient on the final period time dummy estimated without any characteristics covariates but on the same sample from which the hedonic indices are estimated. The regression index also includes indicator variables for the other periods. Hence, any difference between the restricted sample regression index and the regression index is due to the fact that new models are included under the implicit assumption that they are of the same quality as discontinued models. For the unweighted case, for all categories, the (full sample) regression index is higher than the restricted sample regression index. We interpret this result as implying that new models, not accounted for in the restricted sample indices, are entering the market at prices higher than discontinued or extant older models.

The hedonic indices are estimated on the same sample as the standard indices. However, the hedonic regressions include the characteristics covariates, and thus are net of the value of quality changes. In the unweighted case, when vintage is excluded, the hedonic index values are higher than the standard index values. Hence, new models appear to be entering the market with more highly valued characteristics. The hedonic index which includes vintage is usually lower than the corresponding standard index. It is generally lower than the hedonic index which excludes vintage, which supports the hypothesis that vintage provides a "catch-all" variable for those quality improvements which are not elsewhere specified in the regression. It does, however, appear that new higher quality models are entering the market at higher quality adjusted prices. In general, these comparisons among indices derived from the NPD sample alone corroborate the results found for the CPI replication in Table 7, indicating that there is not an anomaly inherent in the CPI sample.

Even when vintage is included in the hedonic regression the hedonic indices remain generally above the standard regression index values. The relationships between the various types of regression-based indices described above for the unweighted case also hold for the weighted least-squares estimates. However, in general the weighted estimates show a smaller price decline than the unweighted estimates. Note that, as expected, the restricted sample regression indices are relatively close to the Tornqvist indices.

In Table 9 the direct hedonic indices are compared to the quality-adjusted CPI values for the period 1998 through January 2000. The hedonic index with vintage excluded is derived from the same regressions that supplied the coefficient values to adjust the CPI, and it is reassuring that the two series are similar. In the last bimonthly period of this comparison, the quality adjusted CPI appears to decrease less quickly than its direct hedonic counterparts, although the statistical significance of these differences is unknown.

Contrary to *a priori* expectations, these empirical results indicate that hedonic quality adjustment may produce higher index values as compared to the case where all new goods are treated as noncomparable. This result seems to be consistent with the conjecture that the introduction of new models is used as an opportunity to raise price. When new models are treated as noncomparable, this price increase remains unaccounted for in the index calculation. Given empirical studies on computers (Stavins (1997)) and television sets in the U.K. (Silver (1998)) and others (Parker (1992)), this model changeover price increase does appear to be a marketing strategy in practice. Not only can producers "piggyback" a pure price increase on new models, it is also possible that the subset of consumers which are most likely to purchase these new models (the "innovators" (Parker (1992)) are less price-sensitive than other consumers and are willing to pay a premium for the new product because it is new.

Consumer audio products do not appear to be unique in this phenomenon. The first results from hedonic models for refrigerators, and some earlier studies of VCRs using published list prices from *Consumer Reports* showed that hedonic quality adjustment could result in a higher index value than its unadjusted counterpart. Among the results to date, hedonic quality adjustment resulted in a 6.5% decline in the index value over a 12-month period for personal computers, a 0.1% decline for a 12-month period for televisions as well as VCRs (Liegey (1999)), and a 0.2% decline for microwave ovens for an 8-month period (Shepler, unpublished draft). All of these studies use expanded samples of CPI data and followed the same methods of using the hedonic coefficients to make adjustments whenever a noncomparable substitution was made in the actual CPI database for a disappeared item. The authors of these studies also noted that the policy of substituting the next most similar item for a disappeared one amounts to substituting the next most close-to-obsolete item, keeping the CPI sample of older vintage than the current market purchase patterns.

IV. Conclusions and Future Research Agenda

Hedonic analysis has long been recommended as a preferred method of quality adjustment of the CPI. For several CPI goods categories, an hedonic approach has been adopted in late 1999 and early 2000, with additional categories of goods and services being evaluated for inclusion in 2000. This is in advance of the next major revision of the CPI in 2002. This paper presents the preliminary results of employing average price and quantity data from a private source to this end for consumer audio electronics products. We have used the hedonic regression coefficients from these data to supply quantitative estimates of quality differences for those situations when substitutions were made in the CPI sample. Also, we have compared the resulting index values to direct hedonic indices calculated from the time dummy variables in the hedonic regressions.

Analysis of these results suggests several interesting empirical issues worthy of further investigation. The quality adjusted indices indicate price decreases over the time period under study, but less so than their unadjusted counterparts. The differences are small, however, so it would be useful to continue empirical investigation, especially during periods where physical changes to audio products are rapid and pronounced. The regression specification with respect to characteristics variables appears to be stable and consistent over time. Interestingly, among the direct hedonic formulas compared, we observed that for all but one product category, the Laspeyres index value is below that of the Paasche index. Altogether, these results support the proposition that new products may be entering the sample at higher quality adjusted prices than those of extant models, an issue that bears further investigation.

Future research will continue to focus on issues of regression specification. Recognizing that the theoretical premise of the hedonic hypothesis is a comparative static model, it is advisable to examine the behavior of characteristics implicit prices in the dynamic market context. The importance of currently unobserved quality attributes in the hedonic model merits more research, especially given that the vintage variable appeared to be important to the numerical results. In addition, alternative approaches to the problem, using discrete choice models as the theoretical basis of analysis may provide promise for empirical application, especially when new goods appear in the market (Berry and Pakes (2000)).

References

Arguea, Nestor, and Cheng Hsiao (1993) "Econometric issues of estimating hedonic price functions," *Journal of Econometrics*, 56, pp.243-267.

Armknecht, Paul (1984) "Quality Adjustment in the CPI and Methods to Improve It,"*Proceedings of the Business and Economic Statistics Section,* American Statistical Association, pp. 57-63.

Armknecht, Paul, and Donald Weyback (1989) "Adjustments for Quality Change in the U.S. Consumer Price Index, *Journal of Official Statistics*, 5, pp. 107-123.

Armknecht, Paul, Brent Moulton, and Kenneth Stewart (1995) "Improvements to the Food at Home, Shelter, and Prescription Drug Indexes in the Consumer Price Index," BLS Working Paper No. 263.

Berry, Steven, and Ariel Pakes (2000) "The Pure Characteristics Discrete Choise Model with Application to Price Indices", preliminary draft.

Court, Andrew (1939) "Hedonic Price Indexes with Automobile Examples," in General Motors Corp*The Dynamics of Automobile Demand,* New York: General Motors Corp., pp. 99-117.

Edmonds, Radcliffe (1985) "Some Evidence on the Intertemporal Stability of Hedonic Price Functions," *Land Economics*, 61, pp. 445-451.

Epple, Dennis (1987) "Hedonic Prices and Implicit Markets: Estimating Demand and Supply Functions for Differentiated Products,"*Journal of Political Economy*, 95, November, pp. 59-80.

Fisher, F., and K. Shell (1972) *The Economic Theory of Price Indices: Two Essays on the Effects of Taste, Quality, and Technological Change.* New York: Academic Press.

Fixler, Dennis (1993) "The Consumer Price Index: underlying concepts and caveats,"*Monthly Labor Review*, 116, December, pp. 3-12.

Fixler, Dennis, Charles Fortuna, and Walter Lane (1999) "The Use of Hedonic Regression to Handle Quality Change: The Experience in the U.S. CPI", paper presented at the fifteh meeting of International Working Group on Price Indices.

Griliches, Zvi (1971) *Price Indexes and Quality Change: Studies in New Methods of Measurement.* Cambridge: Harvard University Press.

Kokoski, Mary (1993) "Quality adjustment of price indexes," *Monthly Labor Review*, 116, December, pp. 34-46.

Kokoski, Mary, and Keith Waehrer (1998) "Hedonics and Quality Adjustment for Price Indices for Consumer Electronics Products," draft presented to NBER Summer Institute Conference on Price Indices, July.

Liegey, Paul (1993) "Adjusting Apparel Indexes in the CPI for Quality Differences", in Foss, M., M. Manser, and A. Young (eds.) *Price Measurements and Their Uses.* National Bureau of Economic Research Studies in Income and Wealth, 57, Chicago: University of Chicago Press, pp. 209-226.

Leigey, Paul (1999) "Developing a Hedonic Regression Model for DVDs in the U.S. CPI" draft paper, available at http://stats.bls.gov.cpihome.htm

Leigey, Paul (2000) "Hedonic Quality Adjustment Methods for Microwave Ovens in the U.S. CPI", unpublished draft.

Liegey, Paul, and Nicole Shepler (1999) "Using Hedonic Methods to Quality Adjust VCR Prices: Plucking a Piece of the US CPI's 'Low Hanging Fruit'?" *Monthly Labor Review*, forthcoming.

Moulton, Brent, Timothy Lafleur, and Karin Moses (1999) "Research on Improved Quality Adjustment in the CPI: The Case of Televisions," *Proceedings of the Fourth Meeting of the International Working Group on Price Indices,* U.S. Dept. of Labor, January, pp. 77-79.

Parker, P. (1992) "Price Elasticity Dynamics Over the Adoption Life Cycle," *Journal of Marketing Research*, August, pp. 358-367.

Rosen, Sherwin (1974) "Hedonic Prices and Hedonic Markets: Product Differentiation in Pure Competition," *Journal of Political Economy*, April, pp. 34-55.

Shepler, Nicole (1999) "Developing a Hedonic Regression Model for Camcorders in the U.S. CPI" draft paper, available at http://stats.bls.gov/cpihome.htm

Shepler, Nicole (2000) "Developing a Hedonic Regression Model for Refrigerators in the U.S. CPI", unpublished draft.

Silver, Mick (1998) "Bias in the Compilation of Consumer Price Indices when Different Models of an Item Coexist," paper presented to the 1998 Ottawa Conference at the U.S. Bureau of Labor Statistics, Washington, D.C, April.

Stavins, J. (1997) "Estimating Demand Elasticities in a Differentiated Product Industry: The Personal Computer Market," *Journal of Economics and Business*, 49, pp. 347-367.

Thompson, William (1999) "Developing a Hedonic Regression Model for VCRs in the U.S. CPI", draft paper, available at http://stats.bls.gov.cpihome.htm

Triplett, Jack (1986) 'The Economic Interpretation of Hedonic Methods,"*Survey of Current Business,* January, pp. 36-40.

Triplett, Jack (1988) "Hedonic functions and hedonic indexes," in*The New Palgraves Dictionary of Economics*, pp. 630-634.

Triplett, Jack (1990) "Hedonic methods in statistical agency environments: an intellectual biopsy," in Berndt, E.R., and J.E. Triplett (eds.) *Fifty years of economic measurement: the Jubilee Conference on Research in Income and Wealth,* NBER Studies in Income and Wealth, Chicago: University of Chicago Press.

Table 1: Table CD Players

		Vintage Included Unweighted	Vintage Included Weight: Average Expenditure Share	Vintage Excluded Unweighted	Vintage Excluded Weight: Average Expenditure Share
	Intercept	5.5618**	5.6480**	5.1852**	5.6122**
		(0.1021)	(0.0902)	(0.1025)	(0.0922)
Load Capacity					
	CD Capacity	0.0018	0.0081**	0.0031*	0.0078**
		(0.0013)	(0.0008)	(0.0014)	(0.0008)
	CD Capacity, Squared	9.34e-6	-4.62e-5**	3.62e-6	-4.71e-5**
		(1.29e-5)	(7.36e-6)	(1.34e-5)	(7.55e-6)
Type of Loader Ref.: Top Loader					
	Drawer Disc Loader	-0.2218*	-0.3660**	-0.2006*	-0.4819**
		(0.0896)	(0.0788)	(0.0930)	(0.0807)
	Front Disc Loader	-0.2109*	-0.4043**	-0.0693	-0.4518**
		(0.0845)	(0.0749)	(0.0872)	(0.0771)
Other Features					
	Remote Control	0.3021**	0.1699**	0.2788**	0.1599**
		(0.0270)	(0.0181)	(0.0280)	(0.0186)
Time Period Ref.: Feb/Mar 1997					
	Apr/May 1997	0.0064	-0.0318	0.0105	-0.0278
		(0.0516)	(0.0583)	(0.0536)	(0.0601)
	June/July 1997	-0.0504	-0.0688	-0.0269	-0.0593
		(0.0505)	(0.0548)	(0.0525)	(0.0564)
	Aug/Sept 1997	-0.0502	-0.0639	-0.0085	-0.0541
		(0.0510)	(0.0546)	(0.0530)	(0.0561)
	Oct/Nov 1997	-0.1275**	-0.1180*	-0.0676	-0.1065
		(0.0517)	(0.0540)	(0.0537)	(0.0555)
	Dec 1997/Jan 1998	-0.1529**	-0.1424**	-0.0808	-0.1290*
		(0.0520)	(0.0535)	(0.0539)	(0.0549)
	Feb/March 1998	-0.1654**	-0.1621**	-0.0693	-0.1388*
		(0.0544)	(0.0530)	(0.0561)	(0.0542)
	Apr/May 1998	-0.1779**	-0.2018**	-0.0666	-0.1736**
		(0.0548)	(0.0526)	(0.0565)	(0.0538)
	June/July 1998	-0.1725**	-0.2357**	-0.0289	-0.1940**
		(0.0554)	(0.0520)	(0.0567)	(0.0530)
	Aug/Sept 1998	-0.2542**	-0.2832**	-0.1014	-0.2335**
		(0.0564)	(0.0520)	(0.0576)	(0.0528)
	Oct/Nov 1998	-0.2673**	-0.3156**	-0.1153*	-0.2572**
		(0.0553)	(0.0516)	(0.0565)	(0.0524)
	Dec 1998/Jan 1999	-0.2609**	-0.3225**	-0.1081	-0.2607**
		(0.0550)	(0.0513)	(0.0561)	(0.0520)
	Feb/March 1999	-0.2721**	-0.3538**	-0.0798	-0.2683**
		(0.0596)	(0.0520)	(0.0603)	(0.0524)
	Apr/May 1999	-0.3515**	-0.4508**	-0.1381*	-0.3304**
		(0.0586)	(0.0509)	(0.0587)	(0.0507)
	June/July 1999	-0.3884**	-0.4991**	-0.1676**	-0.3738**
		(0.0589)	(0.0510)	(0.0586)	(0.0508)
	Aug/Sept 1999	-0.3930**	-0.5101**	-0.1538**	-0.3721**
		(0.0598)	(0.0511)	(0.0590)	(0.0506)
	Oct/Nov 1999	-0.3821**	-0.5232**	-0.1523**	-0.3924**
		(0.0581)	(0.0507)	(0.0573)	(0.0504)
	Dec 1999/Jan 2000	-0.4533**	-0.5426**	-0.2250**	-0.4120**
		(0.0579)	(0.0507)	(0.0571)	(0.0504)

		Vintage Included Unweighted	Vintage Included Weight: Average Expenditure Share	Vintage Excluded Unweighted	Vintage Excluded Weight: Average Expenditure Share
Model Vintage					
	Vintage	-0.0674**	-0.1468**		
		(0.0161)	(0.0115)		
	Vintage, Squared	-0.0088**	0.0311**		
		(0.0031)	(0.0034)		
Summary					
	N	2695	2695	2695	2695
	R-squared	0.4252	0.5665	0.3776	0.5392
	Adjusted R-squared	0.4137	0.5578	0.3656	0.5303
	F-statistic	36.860**	65.113**	31.447**	60.640**

Note: Numbers in parentheses are standard errors.
** Significant at the 99 percent level.
* Significant at the 95 percent level.

Table 2: Portable CD Players

		Vintage Included Unweighted	Vintage Included Weight: Average Expenditure Share	Vintage Excluded Unweighted	Vintage Excluded Weight: Average Expenditure Share
	Intercept	4.6907** (0.0293)	4.2720** (0.0288)	4.3668** (0.0286)	4.1538** (0.0293)
Configuration Ref.: CD Player Only					
	Radio	0.1470** (0.0363)	0.2800** (0.0318)	0.2092** (0.0384)	0.3138** (0.0329)
	Radio and Cassette	0.3167** (0.0148)	0.4087** (0.0126)	0.3184** (0.0157)	0.4096** (0.0130)
Load Capacity					
	CD Capacity	0.0868** (0.0169)	0.2197** (0.0161)	0.0522** (0.0178)	0.1769** (0.0165)
	CD Capacity, Squared	-0.0047* (0.0020)	-0.0171** (0.0017)	-0.0023 (0.0021)	-0.0139** (0.0018)
	CD Capacity, Cubed	3.92e-5* (1.86e-5)	1.52e-4** (1.59e-5)	1.84e-5 (1.97e-5)	1.23e-4** (1.63e-5)
Type of Loader Ref.: Top Loader					
	Drawer Disc Loader	0.1771** (0.0201)	0.1162** (0.0202)	0.1686** (0.0213)	0.1014** (0.0208)
	Front Disc Loader	0.1632** (0.0316)	0.1699** (0.0260)	0.2401** (0.0333)	0.2322** (0.0267)
Other Features					
	Remote Control	0.2600** (0.0107)	0.2331** (0.0087)	0.3004** (0.0113)	0.2508** (0.0089)
	Buffer Memory	0.2936** (0.0151)	0.4762** (0.0141)	0.3611** (0.0158)	0.5002** (0.0146)
	Car Kit	-0.0064 (0.0139)	0.0154 (0.0116)	-0.0354* (0.0147)	0.0033 (0.0120)
Time Period Ref.: Feb/Mar 1997					
	Apr/May 1997	0.0344 (0.0240)	-0.0747** (0.0289)	0.0449 (0.0254)	-0.0700* (0.0299)
	June/July 1997	-0.0395 (0.0237)	-0.0894** (0.0282)	-0.0159 (0.0251)	-0.0794** (0.0292)
	Aug/Sept 1997	-0.1321** (0.0235)	-0.1390** (0.0278)	-0.1040** (0.0249)	-0.1258** (0.0288)
	Oct/Nov 1997	-0.1891** (0.0240)	-0.1844** (0.0278)	-0.1472** (0.0254)	-0.1685** (0.0287)
	Dec 1997/Jan 1998	-0.2341** (0.0240)	-0.2014** (0.0275)	-0.1866** (0.0254)	-0.1810** (0.0284)
	Feb/March 1998	-0.2868** (0.0249)	-0.2699** (0.0270)	-0.2215** (0.0262)	-0.2382** (0.0279)
	Apr/May 1998	-0.3548** (0.0249)	-0.3095** (0.0262)	-0.2590** (0.0261)	-0.2550** (0.0269)
	June/July 1998	-0.4077** (0.0249)	-0.3433** (0.0258)	-0.2922** (0.0259)	-0.2790** (0.0265)
	Aug/Sept 1998	-0.4269** (0.0253)	-0.3688** (0.0257)	-0.2958** (0.0263)	-0.3017** (0.0264)
	Oct/Nov 1998	-0.5215** (0.0253)	-0.4285** (0.0257)	-0.3864** (0.0262)	-0.3605** (0.0263)
	Dec 1998/Jan 1999	-0.4980** (0.0253)	-0.4261** (0.0257)	-0.3641** (0.0263)	-0.3563** (0.0263)
	Feb/March 1999	-0.5160** (0.0267)	-0.5131** (0.0256)	-0.3391** (0.0275)	-0.4098** (0.0261)

		Vintage Included Unweighted	Vintage Included Weight: Average Expenditure Share	Vintage Excluded Unweighted	Vintage Excluded Weight: Average Expenditure Share
	Apr/May 1999	-0.5762** (0.0273)	-0.5727** (0.0254)	-0.3532** (0.0277)	-0.4499** (0.0256)
	June/July 1999	-0.7068** (0.0276)	-0.6590** (0.0253)	-0.4561** (0.0278)	-0.5245** (0.0254)
	Aug/Sept 1999	-0.6793** (0.0278)	-0.6304** (0.0253)	-0.4152** (0.0278)	-0.4875** (0.0252)
	Oct/Nov 1999	-0.6923** (0.0277)	-0.6520** (0.0253)	-0.4129** (0.0274)	-0.5057** (0.0252)
	Dec 1999/Jan 2000	-0.7311** (0.0276)	-0.6537** (0.0252)	-0.4499** (0.0273)	-0.5076** (0.0252)
Model Vintage					
	Vintage	-0.1565** (0.0075)	-0.0992** (0.0061)		
	Vintage, Squared	0.0139** (0.0015)	0.0088** (0.0020)		
Summary					
	N	6709	6709	6709	6709
	R-squared	0.5015	0.5695	0.4403	0.5390
	Adjusted R-squared	0.4974	0.5660	0.4359	0.5354
	F-statistic	123.960**	162.985**	100.682**	149.683**

Note: Numbers in parentheses are standard errors.
** Significant at the 99 percent level.
* Significant at the 95 percent level.

Table 3: Main Stereo Speakers

		Vintage Included Unweighted	Vintage Included Weight: Average Expenditure Share	Vintage Excluded Unweighted	Vintage Excluded Weight: Average Expenditure Share
	Intercept	4.7642** (0.0611)	4.7353** (0.0641)	4.5468** (0.0583)	4.5991** (0.0638)
Configuration Ref.: Single Speaker					
	Pair Configuration	0.2140** (0.0220)	0.1734** (0.0217)	0.2063** (0.0223)	0.1529** (0.0221)
Power Ref.: Not Powered					
	Powered	0.4613** (0.0323)	0.2064** (0.0276)	0.4958** (0.0326)	0.2495** (0.0280)
Speaker Design Ref.: Onwall Speaker					
	Shelf Speaker	-0.4934** (0.0332)	-0.6426** (0.0341)	-0.4823** (0.0223)	-0.6389** (0.0346)
	Floor Speaker	-0.2138** (0.0384)	-0.3875** (0.0375)	-0.2191** (0.0390)	-0.4111** (0.0381)
	Inwall Speaker	-0.3297** (0.0352)	-0.4562** (0.0376)	-0.3249** (0.0357)	-0.4442** (0.0383)
	Other Speaker Design	-0.2740** (0.1059)	-0.4520** (0.0932)	-0.3046** (0.1074)	-0.4858** (0.0949)
Speaker Crossover					
	Main Speaker Crossover	-0.3749** (0.0906)	-0.6303** (0.1790)	-0.3774** (0.0919)	-0.6180** (0.1824)
Woofer Size Ref.: Less than 2 In.					
	4-8 Inch Woofer Size	-0.1350** (0.0396)	-0.0861* (0.0386)	-0.1055** (0.0401)	-0.0630 (0.0393)
	8-12 Inch Woofer Size	0.0555 (0.0435)	0.0873* (0.0419)	0.0885* (0.0441)	0.1088* (0.0427)
	Over 12 Inch Woofer Size	0.2013** (0.0505)	0.2926** (0.0492)	0.2332** (0.0512)	0.2929** (0.0502)
Main Speaker Drivers Ref.: One Driver					
	Two Drivers	0.6107** (0.0857)	0.7524** (0.1767)	0.6178** (0.0869)	0.7648** (0.1801)
	Three Drivers	0.9019** (0.0876)	1.0634** (0.1774)	0.9116** (0.0889)	1.1028** (0.1808)
	Four Drivers	1.2088** (0.0912)	1.4647** (0.1787)	1.2247** (0.0926)	1.4922** (0.1822)
	Five Drivers	1.1358** (0.1036)	1.4281** (0.1829)	1.1448** (0.1051)	1.4337** (0.1864)
	Six Drivers	1.6744** (0.1252)	2.0026** (0.1997)	1.6500** (0.1271)	1.9711** (0.2036)
	Seven Drivers	1.6938** (0.1076)	2.0301** (0.1847)	1.6721** (0.1092)	2.0156** (0.1883)
Other Features					
	Magnetic Shielding	0.1485** (0.0177)	0.2043** (0.0170)	0.1937** (0.0175)	0.2679** (0.0167)
	Weather Proofing	0.0297 (0.0288)	0.1596** (0.0254)	0.0354 (0.0291)	0.1367** (0.0255)
	Mounting Accessories	-0.1234** (0.0257)	-0.2793** (0.0263)	-0.1293** (0.0260)	-0.2734** (0.0268)

		Vintage Included Unweighted	Vintage Included Weight: Average Expenditure Share	Vintage Excluded Unweighted	Vintage Excluded Weight: Average Expenditure Share
	Wireless	0.3293** (0.1191)	0.5251** (0.0928)	0.3477** (0.1209)	0.4853** (0.0945)
Time Period Ref.: Feb/Mar 1997					
	Apr/May 1997	-0.0257 (0.0346)	-0.0132 (0.0349)	-0.0231 (0.0351)	-0.0116 (0.0356)
	June/July 1997	-0.0444 (0.0347)	-0.0321 (0.0348)	-0.0393 (0.0352)	-0.0295 (0.0355)
	Aug/Sept 1997	-0.0493 (0.0346)	-0.0338 (0.0348)	-0.0402 (0.0351)	-0.0300 (0.0355)
	Oct/Nov 1997	-0.0594 (0.0348)	-0.0352 (0.0338)	-0.0419 (0.0353)	-0.0241 (0.0344)
	Dec 1997/Jan 1998	-0.0915** (0.0347)	-0.0535 (0.0337)	-0.0737* (0.0352)	-0.0459 (0.0342)
	Feb/March 1998	-0.1022** (0.0355)	-0.0624 (0.0333)	-0.0749* (0.0359)	-0.0486 (0.0338)
	Apr/May 1998	-0.0807* (0.0355)	-0.0556 (0.0331)	-0.0538 (0.0360)	-0.0403 (0.0336)
	June/July 1998	-0.1045** (0.0357)	-0.0821* (0.0331)	-0.0750* (0.0361)	-0.0647 (0.0336)
	Aug/Sept 1998	-0.1366** (0.0359)	-0.0876** (0.0330)	-0.1018** (0.0364)	-0.0616 (0.0335)
	Oct/Nov 1998	-0.1583** (0.0351)	-0.0909** (0.0325)	-0.1096** (0.0354)	-0.0512 (0.0329)
	Dec 1998/Jan 1999	-0.1497** (0.0351)	-0.0852** (0.0325)	-0.0964** (0.0353)	-0.0412 (0.0328)
	Feb/March 1999	-0.1333** (0.0369)	-0.0790* (0.0331)	-0.0660 (0.0370)	-0.0294 (0.0334)
	Apr/May 1999	-0.1397** (0.0366)	-0.0946** (0.0330)	-0.0702 (0.0366)	-0.0384 (0.0333)
	June/July 1999	-0.1751** (0.0369)	-0.1136** (0.0329)	-0.0949** (0.0367)	-0.0468 (0.0330)
	Aug/Sept 1999	-0.1798** (0.0370)	-0.1449** (0.0330)	-0.0938* (0.0367)	-0.0748* (0.0330)
	Oct/Nov 1999	-0.1666** (0.0363)	-0.1511** (0.0329)	-0.0736* (0.0358)	-0.0736* (0.0328)
	Dec 1999/Jan 2000	-0.1322** (0.0360)	-0.1647** (0.0330)	-0.0362 (0.0354)	-0.0859** (0.0329)
Model Vintage					
	Vintage	-0.0583** (0.0081)	-0.0874 (0.0071)		
	Vintage, Squared	0.0010 (0.0011)	0.0071 (0.0008)		
Summary					
	N	4890	4890	4890	4890
	R-squared	0.7706	0.8254	0.7635	0.8184
	Adjusted R-squared	0.7666	0.8223	0.7594	0.8152
	F-statistic	189.896**	267.205**	186.950**	260.907**

Note: Numbers in parentheses are standard errors.
** Significant at the 99 percent level.
* Significant at the 95 percent level.

28

Table 4: Surround Speakers

		Vintage Included Unweighted	Vintage Included Weight: Average Expenditure Share	Vintage Excluded Unweighted	Vintage Excluded Weight: Average Expenditure Share
	Intercept	5.1297** (0.0869)	5.0156** (0.0766)	4.7739** (0.0868)	4.6962** (0.0725)
Configuration Ref.: Single Speaker					
	Pair Configuration	0.6317** (0.1172)	0.4569** (0.1174)	0.6212** (0.1216)	0.4776** (0.1212)
	Surround Configuration	-0.2020** (0.0648)	-0.2387** (0.0563)	-0.1395* (0.0670)	-0.0932 (0.0566)
Power Ref.: Not Powered					
	Powered	0.5754** (0.0460)	0.4504** (0.0493)	0.6655** (0.0474)	0.5913** (0.0461)
Speaker Type Ref.: Main Speaker					
	Center Speaker	-0.1290* (0.0510)	-0.1601** (0.0567)	-0.1109* (0.0530)	-0.0301 (0.0551)
	Rear Speaker	-0.7253** (0.1332)	-0.1656 (0.1305)	-0.5717** (0.1377)	0.0244 (0.1339)
System Type Ref.: Three-Piece					
	Four-Piece System	0.9006** (0.0842)	0.8885** (0.0607)	0.7133** (0.0864)	0.7067** (0.0530)
	Five-Piece System	0.6918** (0.0882)	0.7145** (0.0636)	0.7251** (0.0914)	0.7677** (0.0655)
	Six-Piece System	0.8087** (0.0657)	0.8592** (0.0541)	0.8442** (0.0681)	0.8502** (0.0553)
	Other System	1.6588** (0.1366)	2.9352** (0.1347)	1.5153** (0.1414)	2.7582** (0.1383)
Surround Speaker Ref.: Other					
	Shelf Speaker	0.1264* (0.0555)	-0.1489** (0.0453)	0.0048 (0.0569)	-0.2191** (0.0456)
	Inwall Speaker	1.4142** (0.1772)	1.5240** (0.2541)	1.5015** (0.1837)	1.6052** (0.2623)
	Onwall Speaker	0.1766* (0.0687)	-0.1214 (0.0703)	0.0846 (0.0708)	-0.1875** (0.0724)
Other Features					
	Magnetic Shielding	0.0408 (0.0318)	0.1093** (0.0273)	0.0674* (0.0330)	0.0906** (0.0282)
	Mounting Accessories	0.0094 (0.0364)	-0.1185** (0.0298)	0.0199 (0.0376)	-0.1199** (0.0299)
	THX Certification	0.3481** (0.0502)	0.2682** (0.0552)	0.3889** (0.0520)	0.2824** (0.0570)
Time Period Ref.: Feb/Mar 1997					
	Apr/May 1997	0.0031 (0.0455)	-0.0097 (0.0421)	0.0041 (0.0472)	-0.0078 (0.0435)
	June/July 1997	-0.0874 (0.0451)	-0.0430 (0.0415)	-0.0841 (0.0468)	-0.0399 (0.0428)
	Aug/Sept 1997	-0.0515 (0.0449)	-0.0478 (0.0412)	-0.0425 (0.0466)	-0.0445 (0.0425)
	Oct/Nov 1997	-0.1107* (0.0451)	-0.0897* (0.0403)	-0.0918* (0.0468)	-0.0763 (0.0416)
	Dec 1997/Jan 1998	-0.0796 (0.0459)	-0.1025* (0.0401)	-0.0537 (0.0476)	-0.0841* (0.0414)

		Vintage Included Unweighted	Vintage Included Weight: Average Expenditure Share	Vintage Excluded Unweighted	Vintage Excluded Weight: Average Expenditure Share
	Feb/March 1998	-0.0996* (0.0479)	-0.1237** (0.0403)	-0.0519 (0.0496)	-0.0970* (0.0416)
	Apr/May 1998	-0.1297** (0.0485)	-0.1178** (0.0404)	-0.0819 (0.0502)	-0.0908* (0.0416)
	June/July 1998	-0.1365** (0.0491)	-0.1356** (0.0405)	-0.0840 (0.0508)	-0.1057* (0.0418)
	Aug/Sept 1998	-0.1194* (0.0482)	-0.1582** (0.0387)	-0.0479 (0.0498)	-0.1045** (0.0398)
	Oct/Nov 1998	-0.1891** (0.0474)	-0.1872** (0.0380)	-0.1020* (0.0489)	-0.1148** (0.0389)
	Dec 1998/Jan 1999	-0.2069** (0.0472)	-0.2070** (0.0380)	-0.1073* (0.0486)	-0.1314** (0.0388)
	Feb/March 1999	-0.2471** (0.0501)	-0.2699** (0.0384)	-0.1297* (0.0513)	-0.1798** (0.0391)
	Apr/May 1999	-0.2308** (0.0505)	-0.2547** (0.0384)	-0.0950 (0.0515)	-0.1564** (0.0390)
	June/July 1999	-0.2550** (0.0511)	-0.2629** (0.0388)	-0.0998 (0.0517)	-0.1529** (0.0392)
	Aug/Sept 1999	-0.2819** (0.0526)	-0.2511** (0.0390)	-0.1061* (0.0529)	-0.1317** (0.0393)
	Oct/Nov 1999	-0.3187** (0.0498)	-0.2822** (0.0384)	-0.1258* (0.0494)	-0.1561** (0.0384)
	Dec 1999/Jan 2000	-0.2538** (0.0498)	-0.3281** (0.0380)	-0.0531 (0.0492)	-0.2048** (0.0382)
Model Vintage					
	Vintage	-0.1073** (0.0130)	-0.1058** (0.0105)		
	Vintage, Squared	-0.0008 (0.0024)	0.0074** (0.0026)		
Summary					
	N	3049	3049	3049	3049
	R-squared	0.7700	0.8421	0.7521	0.8315
	Adjusted R-squared	0.7638	0.8379	0.7455	0.8271
	F-statistic	124.228**	197.918**	115.494**	187.965**

Note: Numbers in parentheses are standard errors.
** Significant at the 99 percent level.
* Significant at the 95 percent level.

Table 5: Receivers

		Vintage Included Unweighted	Vintage Included Weight: Average Expenditure Share	Vintage Excluded Unweighted	Vintage Excluded Weight: Average Expenditure Share
	Intercept	4.7784**	4.3229**	4.2288**	3.8897**
		(0.0757)	(0.0785)	(0.0820)	(0.0841)
Watts Capability					
	Watts per Channel	0.0111**	0.0117**	0.0108**	0.0109**
		(0.0003)	(0.0003)	(0.0003)	(0.0004)
Radio Tuner Ref.: Analog Tuner					
	Digital Tuner	-0.1423**	-0.0888*	-0.2870**	-0.1193**
		(0.0468)	(0.0350)	(0.0520)	(0.0383)
Other Features					
	Graphic Equalizer	-0.0332	-0.0513	0.0740	0.1202**
		(0.0374)	(0.0344)	(0.0407)	(0.0368)
	Remote Control	-0.0348	0.1690**	0.1164*	0.3116**
		(0.0444)	(0.0546)	(0.0492)	(0.0594)
	Video Switching	0.4433**	0.5717**	0.5062**	0.6749**
		(0.0269)	(0.0261)	(0.0298)	(0.0277)
	THX Certification	0.8526**	0.6345**	0.9042**	0.6979**
		(0.0337)	(0.0319)	(0.0377)	(0.0348)
Surround Decoder					
	Dolby Pro Logic	-0.2347**	-0.4618**	-0.2895**	-0.5822**
		(0.0191)	(0.0170)	(0.0207)	(0.0173)
	Dolby Digital	0.3395**	0.0896**	0.4184**	0.0577**
		(0.0234)	(0.0173)	(0.0258)	(0.0177)
Time Period Ref.: Feb/Mar 1997					
	Apr/May 1997	0.1479**	0.3095**	0.2022**	0.4268**
		(0.0385)	(0.0514)	(0.0429)	(0.0560)
	June/July 1997	0.0867*	0.2482**	0.1723**	0.3889**
		(0.0381)	(0.0500)	(0.0425)	(0.0544)
	Aug/Sept 1997	0.0383	0.1930**	0.1313**	0.3324**
		(0.0376)	(0.0492)	(0.0420)	(0.0536)
	Oct/Nov 1997	0.0150	0.1787**	0.1300**	0.3392**
		(0.0380)	(0.0485)	(0.0424)	(0.0526)
	Dec 1997/Jan 1998	-0.0289	0.1466**	0.0995*	0.3183**
		(0.0381)	(0.0481)	(0.0424)	(0.0522)
	Feb/March 1998	-0.0312	0.1044*	0.1350**	0.2949**
		(0.0393)	(0.0478)	(0.0437)	(0.0518)
	Apr/May 1998	-0.1231**	0.0271	0.0658	0.2428**
		(0.0393)	(0.0472)	(0.0435)	(0.0510)
	June/July 1998	-0.1274**	0.0024	0.0874*	0.2401**
		(0.0393)	(0.0468)	(0.0433)	(0.0504)
	Aug/Sept 1998	-0.2318**	-0.0660	-0.0005	0.1793**
		(0.0395)	(0.0465)	(0.0434)	(0.0499)
	Oct/Nov 1998	-0.2437**	-0.0911*	0.0064	0.1825**
		(0.0390)	(0.0457)	(0.0427)	(0.0488)
	Dec 1998/Jan 1999	-0.2706**	-0.1121*	-0.0070	0.1771**
		(0.0391)	(0.0455)	(0.0428)	(0.0484)
	Feb/March 1999	-0.3666**	-0.1826**	-0.0530	0.1417**
		(0.0408)	(0.0456)	(0.0443)	(0.0482)
	Apr/May 1999	-0.4163**	-0.2667**	-0.0510	0.0813**
		(0.0412)	(0.0452)	(0.0441)	(0.0474)
	June/July 1999	-0.4793**	-0.3388**	-0.0681	0.0434

31

		Vintage Included Unweighted	Vintage Included Weight: Average Expenditure Share	Vintage Excluded Unweighted	Vintage Excluded Weight: Average Expenditure Share
		(0.0416)	(0.0450)	(0.0439)	(0.0466)
	Aug/Sept 1999	-0.4871**	-0.3557**	-0.0664	0.0399
		(0.0412)	(0.0448)	(0.0433)	(0.0462)
	Oct/Nov 1999	-0.4886**	-0.3557**	-0.0614	0.0390
		(0.0403)	(0.0446)	(0.0421)	(0.0460)
	Dec 1999/Jan 2000	-0.5511**	-0.4061**	-0.1224**	-0.0115
		(0.0404)	(0.0447)	(0.0422)	(0.0461)
Model Vintage					
	Vintage	-0.2138**	-0.1801**		
		(0.0110)	(0.0101)		
	Vintage, Squared	0.0144**	0.0063		
		(0.0024)	(0.0035)		
Summary					
	N	3781	3781	3781	3781
	R-squared	0.7381	0.7902	0.6710	0.7484
	Adjusted R-squared	0.7346	0.7874	0.6668	0.7452
	F-statistic	210.267**	281.008**	158.582**	231.311**

Note: Numbers in parentheses are standard errors.
** Significant at the 99 percent level.
* Significant at the 95 percent level.

		Vintage Included Unweighted	Vintage Included Weight: Average Expenditure Share	Vintage Excluded Unweighted	Vintage Excluded Weight: Average Expenditure Share
	Intercept	5.9341**	6.1965**	5.4880**	6.1535**
		(0.0820)	(0.0777)	(0.0927)	(0.0873)
Product Type Ref.: Micro, One-Piece					
	Midi, One Piece	-0.8355**	-0.9031**	-1.2507**	-1.4061**
		(0.1725)	(0.1409)	(0.1991)	(0.1531)
	Midi, With Cassette	-0.4559**	-0.6131**	-0.6204**	-0.7285**
		(0.0596)	(0.0513)	(0.0683)	(0.0577)
	Midi, Two Pieces	-0.4387**	-0.6419**	-0.6956**	-0.6455**
		(0.0851)	(0.0874)	(0.0975)	(0.0990)
	Mini, One Piece	-0.4217**	-0.4665**	-0.4551**	-0.5074**
		(0.0698)	(0.0542)	(0.0808)	(0.0614)
	Mini, With Cassette	-0.5814**	-0.7238**	-0.6976**	-0.7817**
		(0.0495)	(0.0413)	(0.0567)	(0.0467)
	Mini, Two Pieces	-0.3307**	-0.4089**	-0.6339**	-0.6795**
		(0.0552)	(0.0609)	(0.0622)	(0.0663)
	Mini, Three Pieces	-0.6677**	-0.7778**	-0.8490**	-0.7543**
		(0.1038)	(0.0695)	(0.1198)	(0.0788)
	Micro, With Cassette	-0.5111**	-0.4262**	-0.5612**	-0.4286**
		(0.0519)	(0.0414)	(0.0591)	(0.0468)
	Micro, Two Pieces	-0.0259	0.0361	-0.0100	0.0208
		(0.0794)	(0.0692)	(0.0919)	(0.0784)
	Micro, Separate Amp.	0.6255**	0.6393**	0.2134	0.3307*
		(0.1064)	(0.1234)	(0.1216)	(0.1390)
Watts Capability					
	Watts per Channel	0.0002	0.0009**	0.0009**	0.0013**
		(0.0002)	(0.0002)	(0.0002)	(0.0002)
Subwoofer System					
	Subwoofer System	0.1152**	0.0122	0.2058**	0.0117
		(0.0361)	(0.0254)	(0.0413)	(0.0286)
Cassette Deck Ref.: Single Cassette					
	Double Cassette	-0.2186**	-0.0642*	-0.3559**	-0.1577**
		(0.0362)	(0.0281)	(0.0414)	(0.0305)
Capacity					
	CD Capacity	0.0221**	0.0253**	0.0159**	0.0301**
		(0.0037)	(0.0048)	(0.0043)	(0.0055)
	CD Capacity, Squared	-0.0003**	-0.0005**	-0.0002**	-0.0005**
		(0.0001)	(0.0001)	(0.0001)	(0.0001)
Features					
	Digital Signal Processing	0.1843**	-0.0172	0.1810**	-0.0654*
		(0.0372)	(0.0233)	(0.0425)	(0.0262)
	Remote Control	0.0427	-0.0346	0.1859**	-0.0390
		(0.0493)	(0.0533)	(0.0564)	(0.0600)
	Surround Sound	0.0832**	0.0620**	0.2271**	0.0585**
		(0.0269)	(0.0191)	(0.0303)	(0.0214)
	Woofer Size	0.0791**	0.0372**	0.0686**	0.0029
		(0.0106)	(0.0089)	(0.0123)	(0.0099)
	Dolby Surround Sound	0.1841**	0.2206**	0.1604**	0.2179**
		(0.0324)	(0.0238)	(0.0375)	(0.0270)
Speakers Ref.: 4-Way Speakers					
	2-Way Speakers	0.2352**	0.2138**	0.2448**	0.2935**

		Vintage Included Unweighted	Vintage Included Weight: Average Expenditure Share	Vintage Excluded Unweighted	Vintage Excluded Weight: Average Expenditure Share
		(0.0329)	(0.0293)	(0.0377)	(0.0324)
	3-Way Speakers	0.3232**	0.4752**	0.3303**	0.6120**
		(0.0371)	(0.0365)	(0.0421)	(0.0396)
	4-Way Speakers	0.3304**	0.7348**	0.4173**	0.8737**
		(0.0636)	(0.0542)	(0.0734)	(0.0601)
Time Period Ref.: Feb/Mar 1997					
	Apr/May 1997	-0.0015	-0.0292	0.0106	-0.0179
		(0.0414)	(0.0431)	(0.0480)	(0.0489)
	June/July 1997	-0.0340	-0.0866*	0.0085	-0.0432
		(0.0416)	(0.0411)	(0.0482)	(0.0466)
	Aug/Sept 1997	-0.0717	-0.1147**	-0.0127	-0.0603
		(0.0414)	(0.0415)	(0.0479)	(0.0470)
	Oct/Nov 1997	-0.1784**	-0.1830**	-0.0985*	-0.1282*
		(0.0432)	(0.0451)	(0.0499)	(0.0510)
	Dec 1997/Jan 1998	-0.1484**	-0.2028**	-0.0594	-0.1347**
		(0.0431)	(0.0442)	(0.0498)	(0.0500)
	Feb/March 1998	-0.1156*	-0.2285**	0.0216	-0.1383**
		(0.0466)	(0.0445)	(0.0536)	(0.0502)
	Apr/May 1998	-0.2415**	-0.2730**	-0.0761	-0.1740**
		(0.0461)	(0.0436)	(0.0528)	(0.0492)
	June/July 1998	-0.2848**	-0.3764**	-0.0714	-0.2335**
		(0.0464)	(0.0419)	(0.0528)	(0.0469)
	Aug/Sept 1998	-0.3348**	-0.3677**	-0.0921	-0.2168**
		(0.0469)	(0.0415)	(0.0531)	(0.0464)
	Oct/Nov 1998	-0.3818**	-0.4137**	-0.1221*	-0.2652**
		(0.0460)	(0.0413)	(0.0519)	(0.0462)
	Dec 1998/Jan 1999	-0.4043**	-0.4236**	-0.1326*	-0.2748**
		(0.0462)	(0.0412)	(0.0520)	(0.0461)
	Feb/March1999	-0.5352**	-0.5912**	-0.2151**	-0.4005**
		(0.0495)	(0.0408)	(0.0553)	(0.0452)
	Apr/May 1999	-0.5680**	-0.6365**	-0.2267**	-0.4305**
		(0.0501)	(0.0407)	(0.0557)	(0.0449)
	June/July 1999	-0.6797**	-0.7271**	-0.3008**	-0.5075**
		(0.0526)	(0.0410)	(0.0582)	(0.0450)
	Aug/Sept 1999	-0.7338**	-0.7104**	-0.3190**	-0.4822**
		(0.0519)	(0.0409)	(0.0566)	(0.0447)
	Oct/Nov 1999	-0.7748**	-0.7449**	-0.3178**	-0.4967**
		(0.0534)	(0.0412)	(0.0573)	(0.0449)
	Dec 1999/Jan 2000	-0.7769**	-0.7683**	-0.3599**	-0.5299**
		(0.0504)	(0.0410)	(0.0544)	(0.0447)
Model Vintage					
	Vintage	-0.2295**	-0.1780**		
		(0.0165)	(0.0117)		
	Vintage, Squared	0.0108**	0.0024		
		(0.0033)	(0.0039)		
Summary					
	N	1762	1762	1762	1762
	R-squared	0.7693	0.9012	0.6892	0.8729
	Adjusted R-squared	0.7604	0.8974	0.6777	0.8682
	F-statistic	86.994**	237.955**	59.765**	185.069**

Note: Numbers in parentheses are standard errors.
** Significant at the 99 percent level.
* Significant at the 95 percent level.

34

Table 7: CPI Quality Adjusted by NPD Regression Coefficients

Period	Published Index	Month-to-Month Change	Quality Adjusted Index	Month-to-Month Change	Number of Quality Adjusted Quotes	Number of Price Quotes
9712	100.00	---	100.00	---	---	---
9801	99.47	0.99	99.52	1.00	3	158
9802	98.34	0.99	98.81	0.99	2	140
9803	98.71	1.00	97.85	0.99	5	152
9804	98.29	1.00	98.33	1.00	4	166
9805	97.26	0.99	96.89	0.99	3	187
9806	96.31	0.99	96.01	0.99	2	165
9807	95.79	1.00	95.72	1.00	4	170
9808	95.22	0.99	95.05	0.99	2	167
9809	95.53	1.00	96.36	1.01	12	186
9810	95.22	1.00	94.89	0.98	9	164
9811	93.40	0.98	93.03	0.98	4	186
9812	92.62	0.99	92.42	0.99	2	171
9901	96.47	1.04	96.32	1.04	4	183
9902	95.47	0.99	95.50	0.99	4	162
9903	95.38	1.00	95.93	1.00	3	207
9904	94.82	0.99	95.54	1.00	7	167
9905	93.50	0.99	94.51	0.99	7	205
9906	92.50	0.99	92.31	0.98	4	172
9907	92.08	1.00	92.19	1.00	7	183
9908	91.38	0.99	91.43	0.99	8	153
9909	89.74	0.98	91.06	1.00	6	218
9910	89.35	1.00	89.25	0.98	3	216
9911	89.54	1.00	89.19	1.00	4	225
9912	88.99	0.99	89.16	1.00	0	190
0001	89.26	1.00	89.15	1.00	3	265

Table 8
February/March 1997=100
Direct Hedonic Price Indices: February/March 1997 to December 1999/January 2000

	Table CD Players	Portable CD Players	Main Stereo Speakers	Surround Speakers	Receivers	Shelf Systems
Standard Indices						
Laspeyres	57.54	57.52	86.39	66.20	58.78	40.20
Paasche	94.73	41.48	96.89	89.50	84.43	37.15
Geometric Mean	53.23	51.83	83.17	61.21	54.30	37.63
Fisher	73.83	48.85	91.49	76.98	70.45	38.65
Tornqvist	54.45	47.60	89.52	67.16	56.10	37.66
Indices (Unweighted)						
Restricted Sample Regression Index (No Quality Adjustment)	76.36	55.75	84.39	79.79	59.48	45.80
Full Sample Regression Index (No Quality Adjustment)	98.79	68.91	112.48	133.61	100.57	105.44
Full Sample Hedonic Index, Vintage Excluded	79.85	63.77	96.45	94.82	88.48	69.77
Full Sample Hedonic Index, Vintage Included	63.55	48.14	87.62	77.58	57.63	45.98
Indices with Average Expenditure Share Weights						
Restricted Sample Regression Index (No Quality Adjustment)	67.76	52.97	89.15	69.35	59.55	41.30
Full Sample Regression Index (No Quality Adjustment)	71.90	63.10	96.03	112.07	95.27	41.00
Full Sample Hedonic Index, Vintage Excluded	66.23	60.19	91.77	81.48	98.86	58.87
Full Sample Hedonic Index, Vintage Included	58.12	52.01	84.82	72.03	66.63	46.38

Table 9
Dec 1997/Jan 1998=100
Comparison of Quality Adjusted CPI to Direct Hedonic Indexes

	Feb/March 1998	April/May 1998	June/July 1998	August/Sept 1998	Oct/Nov 1998	Dec 1998/Jan 1999
Full Sample Hedonic Index, Unweighted, Vintage Excluded	100.75	97.53	97.41	94.67	91.83	91.75
Full Sample Hedonic Index, Unweighted, Vintage Included	99.46	93.71	91.71	87.99	84.59	84.17
Quality Adjusted CPI	98.33	97.61	95.87	95.71	93.96	94.37

	Feb/March 1999	April/May 1999	June/July 1999	August/Sept 1999	Oct/Nov 1999	Dec 1999/Jan 2000
Full Sample Hedonic Index, Unweighted, Vintage Excluded	91.27	90.55	86.28	87.33	87.70	86.15
Full Sample Hedonic Index, Unweighted, Vintage Included	81.20	78.48	73.02	72.93	72.65	71.52
Quality Adjusted CPI	95.71	95.02	92.25	91.25	89.22	89.15

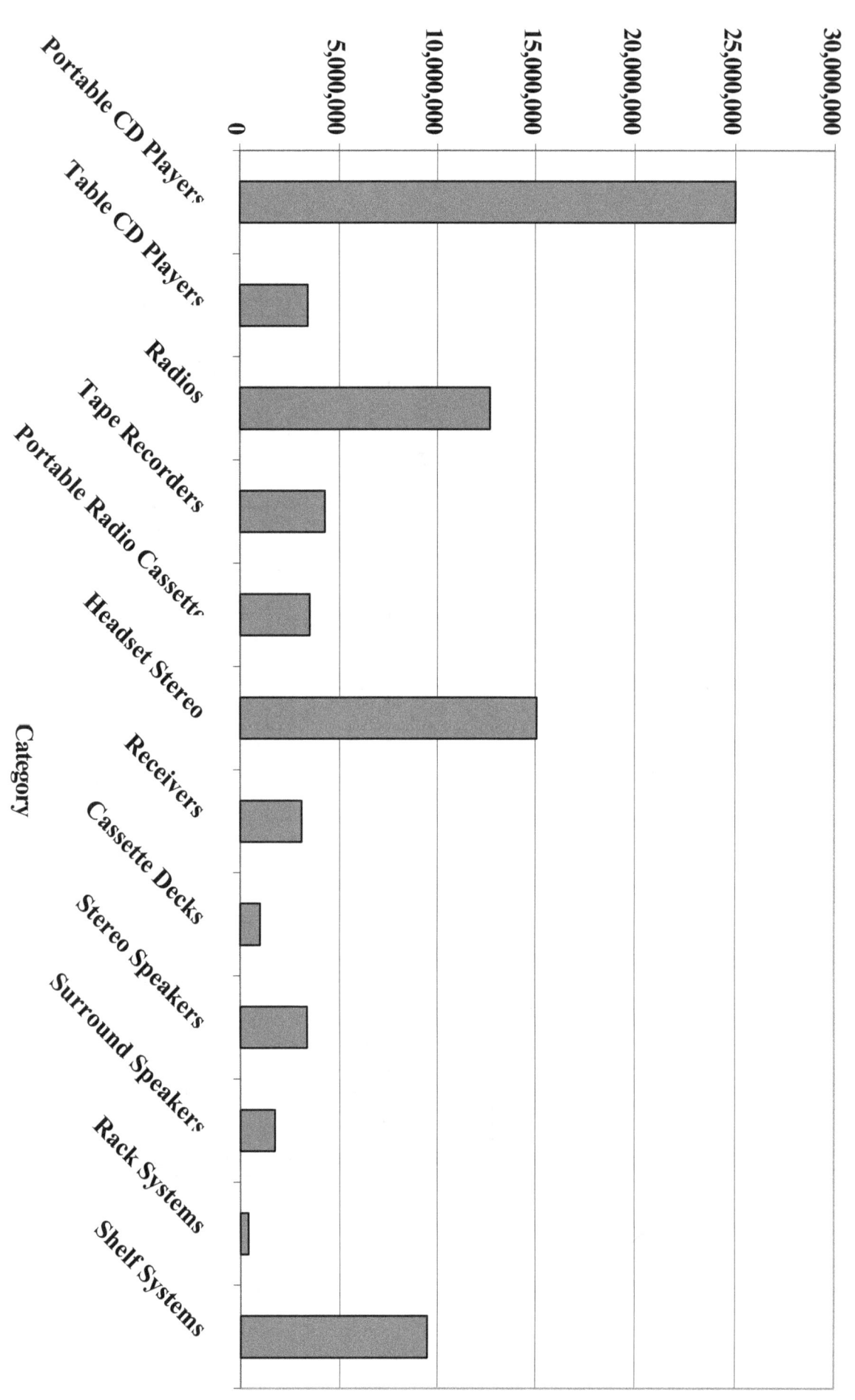

Figure 1: Units Sold Per NPD Category (February/March 1997 - February/March 1999)

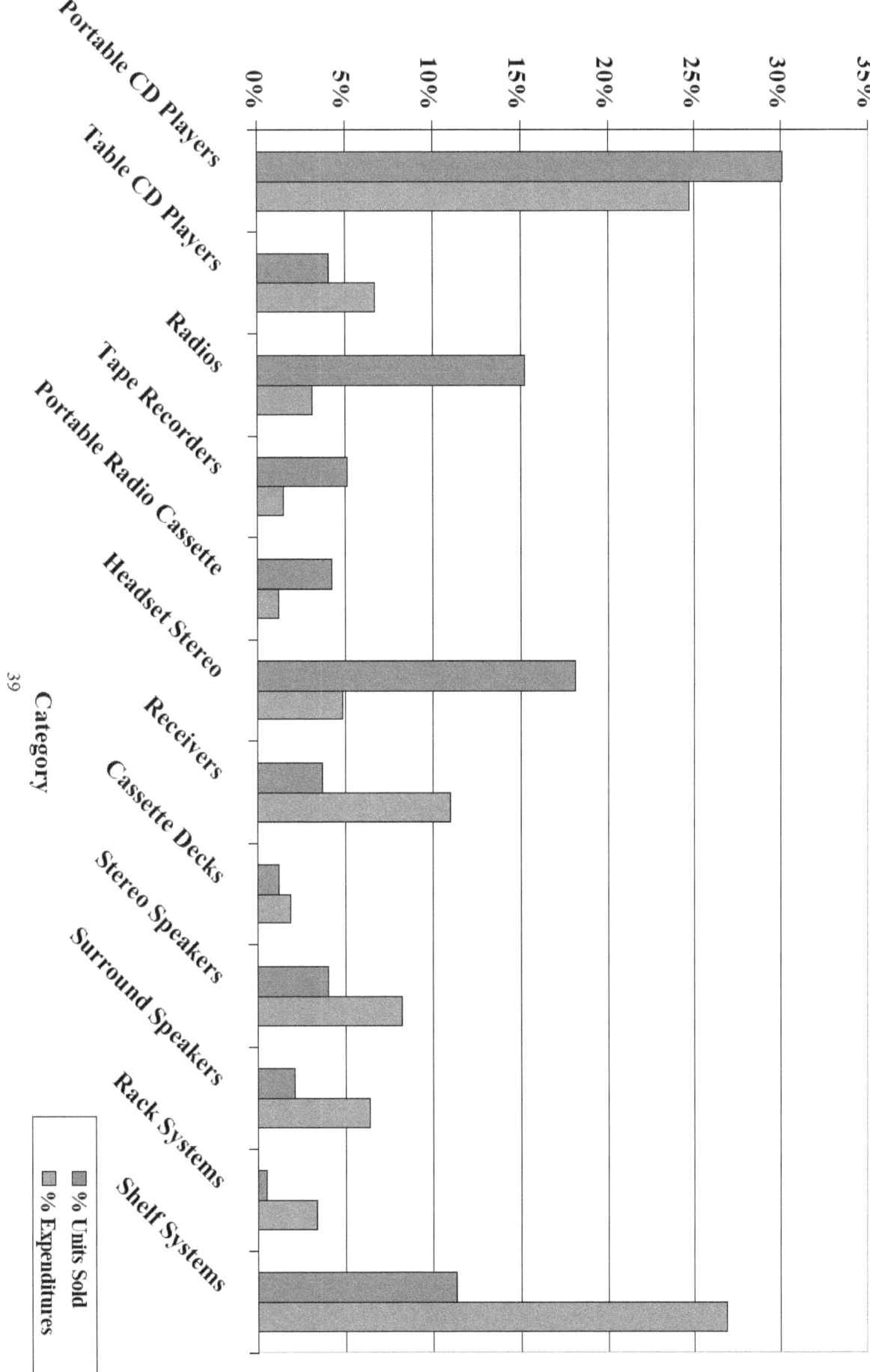

Figure 2: Relative Units Sold and Expenditures, NPD Data

39

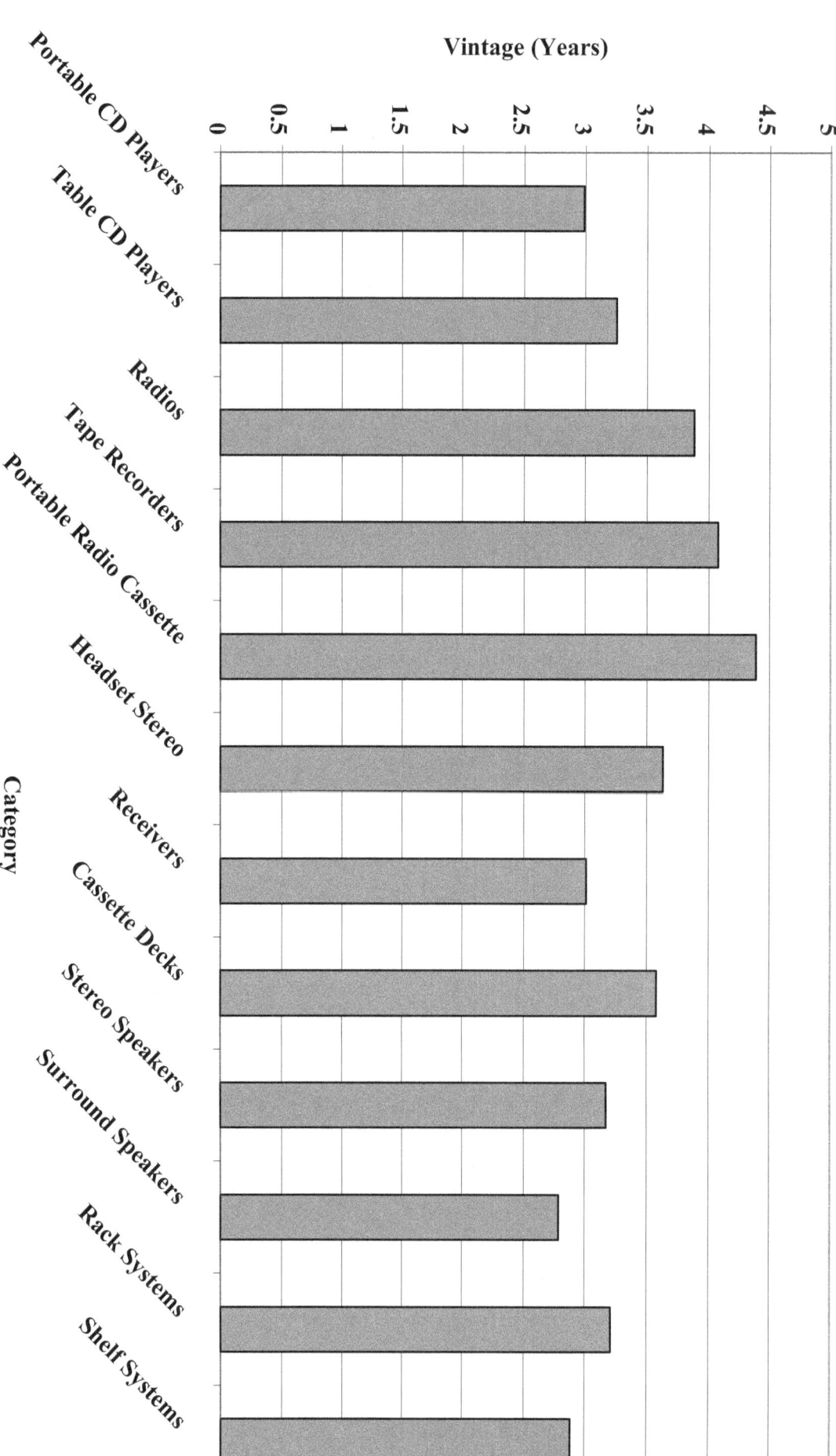

Figure 3: Average Vintage, as of March 1999

40

Table A.1: Regression Coefficients for Brand Names
Unweighted Full Sample Regressions, Vintage Included
Reference Brand: SONY

	Table CD Players	Portable CD Players	Main Stereo Speakers	Surround Speakers	Receivers	Shelf Systems
Acoustic Research			0.7508** (0.0650)	0.5641** (0.1477)		
Adcom	1.1927** (0.1489)					
ADS			1.4482** (0.3935)			
Advent			0.1885** (0.0541)	-0.6076** (0.0975)		
Aiwa	0.0469 (0.1342)	-0.1694** (0.0157)		-0.7220** (0.1003)	-0.2710** (0.0780)	-0.2744** (0.0489)
Alaron		-1.0536** (0.1453)				
Altec			-0.3787** (0.0769)	-0.4561** (0.1924)		
Audiovox		-0.9704** (0.1624)	0.0914 (0.1821)	-0.2482* (0.1275)		
B&K					1.7436** (0.1014)	
B&W			2.0149** (0.0516)	1.2722** (0.0902)		
Bang and Olufsen	0.9252** (0.4423)		2.2397** (0.0797)			
BIC			0.3313** (0.0892)	0.0487 (0.1268)		
Bose			1.0727** (0.0595)	0.5210** (0.0899)		1.5171** (0.0887)
Boston Acoustics			0.9309** (0.0496)	0.7110** (0.0818)		
California Audio	0.8425** (0.1821)					
Canton				1.0331** (0.2627)		
Carver	0.6329** (0.1487)				1.2044** (0.1829)	
Casio		-0.3098** (0.0818)				
Celestion			0.7307** (0.1145)	0.0658 (0.1808)		
Cerwin Vega			0.4448** (0.0630)	0.2531** (0.0895)		
Craig		-0.5331** (0.0332)				
Definitive			0.8991** (0.0620)	1.1715** (0.0830)		
Denon	0.3725** (0.0498)			0.1276 (0.2628)	0.6034** (0.0271)	0.6393** (0.0685)
Emerson		-0.4115** (0.0584)				-0.4113* (0.2190)
Energy			1.3530** (0.0653)	0.5303** (0.1054)		
Fisher	-0.2727** (0.0621)	-0.2010** (0.0221)	-0.3248 (0.3931)	-1.1974** (0.3350)	-0.4663** (0.0501)	0.0311 (0.0552)
General Electric		-0.8763** (0.3241)				-1.0385** (0.0912)
Granprix		-0.4944** (0.0321)				
Harman Kardon	0.1494* (0.0900)				0.7291** (0.0360)	0.7614** (0.1274)
Infinity			0.7500** (0.0476)	0.3495** (0.0806)		
JBL			0.4234**	0.1692**		0.3919**

	Table CD Players		Portable CD Players		Main Stereo Speakers		Surround Speakers		Receivers		Shelf Systems	
					(0.0464)		(0.0760)				(0.0966)	
Jensen					-0.5600	**	-1.1529	**				
					(0.1074)		(0.1361)					
JVC	-0.2796	**	-0.1040	**			-0.8700	**	-0.2842	**	0.0501	
	(0.0406)		(0.0167)				(0.2309)		(0.0270)		(0.0330)	
Kash Gold			0.2256	**								
			(0.0906)									
KEF					1.4686	**	1.2250	**				
					(0.0550)		(0.1057)					
Kenwood	-0.2845	**	-0.2088	**	-0.0892		-0.3060	**	-0.1896	**	-0.0046	
	(0.0390)		(0.0244)		(0.0895)		(0.0918)		(0.0248)		(0.0477)	
KLH					-1.3279	**	-0.6245	**				
					(0.0766)		(0.1465)					
Klipsch					1.0142	**	0.5931	**				
					(0.0478)		(0.0788)					
Koss			-0.2621	**							-0.6589	**
			(0.0302)								(0.1041)	
Krell	1.9713	**										
	(0.3207)											
Lenoxx			-0.5120	**								
			(0.1327)									
M&K					2.1508	**	1.3169	**				
					(0.0914)		(0.0884)					
Magnavox	-0.6827	**	-0.1995	**			-0.9045	**	-0.0722		-0.2463	**
	(0.0823)		(0.0182)				(0.1559)		(0.2186)		(0.0600)	
Marantz	0.5306	**							0.7734	**	0.4586	**
	(0.0715)								(0.0447)		(0.1580)	
Martin Logan					2.7095	**	2.5872	**				
					(0.0862)		(0.1247)					
McIntosh							1.9685	**				
							(0.1519)					
Memorex			-0.5250	**								
			(0.1233)									
Meridian	3.0683	**			2.4800	**	2.6593	**				
	(0.2562)				(0.2044)		(0.1963)					
Mirage					1.0915	**	0.8990	**				
					(0.0593)		(0.0819)					
Mission					0.6957	**	0.2228					
					(0.0649)		(0.1454)					
Mitsubishi	0.1353				1.1184	**	0.3366	**	0.4975	**		
	(0.1575)				(0.2800)		(0.1007)		(0.0593)			
MTC	0.4820											
	(0.4510)											
MTX					-0.0059		-0.2111					
					(0.0725)		(0.1503)					
NAD	0.4435	**							2.0082	**		
	(0.0912)								(0.1713)			
Nakamichi	1.1127	**							1.3945	**		
	(0.1421)								(0.3102)			
Newtech			-0.4925	**								
			(0.0717)									
NHT					0.6946	**	0.5715	**				
					(0.1311)		(0.2327)					
Niles					0.9222	**						
					(0.0649)							
Onkyo	0.1686	**	-0.2892	**			-0.1508		0.3964	**	0.3867	**
	(0.0521)		(0.1456)				(0.1937)		(0.0279)		(0.0726)	
Panasonic	-0.3134	**	-0.1125	**					0.0709		-0.0650	
	(0.1310)		(0.0151)						(0.1396)		(0.0514)	
Paradigm					1.1263	**	0.9519	**				
					(0.0882)		(0.1036)					
Phase Tech					1.2382	**	0.4816	**				
					(0.0999)		(0.1455)					
Philips	0.4605	**	-0.5106	**			-0.8583	*	-0.1772			
	(0.1823)		(0.1087)				(0.4411)		(0.1390)			

42

	Table CD Players	Portable CD Players	Main Stereo Speakers	Surround Speakers	Receivers	Shelf Systems
Pioneer	-0.0100 (0.0325)	0.3451 (0.7183)	-0.4989** (0.0597)	-0.4578** (0.0842)	-0.1502** (0.0217)	0.0127 (0.0394)
Pioneer Electech			1.9669** (0.3953)			
Polk			0.8673** (0.0477)	0.6994** (0.0783)		
Polyflame		0.5786* (0.3240)				
RCA	-0.7437** (0.0992)	-0.3371** (0.0197)	-0.6318** (0.2803)	-0.8544** (0.1361)	0.4453** (0.1730)	-0.3915** (0.0445)
Recoton			0.3863** (0.1577)	0.0473 (0.1413)		
Rock Solid			1.2410** (0.0802)			
Rockustics			1.3197** (0.0867)			
Rotel	0.8977** (0.1985)				0.9466** (0.3118)	
Samsung						-0.2611 (0.3083)
Sansui	-0.8506* (0.4417)					
Sanyo		-0.4158** (0.0288)				0.2439 (0.1578)
Sharp		-0.3144** (0.0305)				-0.1845** (0.0468)
Sherwood	-0.5394 (0.4413)				-0.2942* (0.1553)	
Snell			1.2873** (0.3940)			
Sonance			0.9820** (0.0805)			
Soundesign						-0.8593** (0.0625)
Speakercraft			0.5702** (0.2028)			
Stereostone			0.2406* (0.1420)			
Sumiko			2.5607** (0.0713)	1.5772** (0.1347)		
Symphonics	-0.8845** (0.1486)					
Teac	-0.6129** (0.1991)					
Technics	-0.2931** (0.0377)		-0.2434** (0.0631)	-0.4114** (0.0926)	-0.2853** (0.0249)	0.4320** (0.0662)
Toshiba					-0.0190 (0.3090)	
Venturer		-0.5422** (0.1628)				
Velodyne				1.5598** (0.0885)		
Wilson		-0.6885** (0.1502)				
Yamaha	0.0287 (0.0429)		-0.5201** (0.0573)	-0.3598** (0.0782)	0.3824** (0.0236)	0.5024** (0.0538)
Zenith						-0.1038 (0.1296)

Note: Numbers in parentheses are standard errors.
** Significant at the 99 percent level.
* Significant at the 95 percent level.

Bureau of Labor Statistics
Consumer Price Index - ELI Checklist

Collection
Period: __ __ __ __

Outlet
Number: __ __ __ __ __ __ __

Quote
Code: __ __ __

Arranging
Code: __ __ __ __

ELI No./
Cluster title
RA051 AUDIO COMPONENTS, RADIOS, TAPE RECORDERS/PLAYERS, OTHER   code **01**

Item Availability: 1-AVAILABLE   2-ELI NOT SOLD   3-INIT INCOMPLETE Purpose of
Checklist: 1-INIT   2-INIT COMPL   3-SPEC CORR   4-SUB   5-REINIT 6-CHECK
REV_____

____

CURRENT PERIOD   SALES TAX

Price _ _ _ _ _ _ . _ _ _   Included: YES   NO

Type of Price: REG   SALE

YEAR-ROUND in-season: JAN FEB MAR APR MAY JUN JUL AUG SEP OCT NOV DEC

Respondent: Location:

Field Message:

CLUSTER 01 - RADIOS, PHONOGRAPHS AND TAPE RECORDERS/PLAYERS

TYPE

A1 Radio, tape recorder/
    player combination
A2 Radio, tape player
    Combination
A3 Radio
A4 Tape recorder/player
A5 Tape player

BRAND

B99 _____

MODEL NUMBER

C99 _____

STYLE
D1 Personal portable
    music system
D2 Portable (carry about)

NUMBER OF TAPE UNITS
K1 Single tape unit
K2 Dual tape unit

TYPE OF TAPE USED
M1 Standard cassette
M99 Other,

_____

FEATURES
N1 Headphones included as
    standard equipment
P1 Clock radio, digital
P2 Clock radio, analog face
Q1 One tone control
Q2 Two tone controls
Q99 Other _____

S1 Variable tone control(s)
S2 Switchable tone controls
T1 Built-in microphone(s)

D3 Table model

RADIO RECEIVING CAPABILITIES
  E1 FM stereo
  E2 FM monaural
  F1 AM stereo
  F2 AM monaural
  G99 Short wave band(s),
     number, _____
  H1 Weather band
  I1 TV band
  J99 Other(s),

     _____

T2 External microphone(s) included
    as standard equipment
U1 Local/DX switch
V99 Other,

     _____

W99 Other,

     _____

X99 Other,

     _____

POWER
  AA1 AC, house current
  AB1 DC, Rechargeable battery(ies)
     included as standard equipment
  AB2 DC, nonrechargeable battery(ies)
     equipment included as standard
  AB3 DC, battery(ies)--not included
  AC99 Other,

     _____

Collection Period: __ __ __ __	Outlet Number: __ __ __ __ __ __ __	Quote Code: __ __ __	Arranging Code: __ __ __ __

___

ELI No./
title **RA051 COMPONENTS AND OTHER SOUND EQUIPMENT**

Cluster
code **02**

___

Item Availability: 1-AVAILABLE   2-ELI NOT SOLD   3-INIT INCOMPLETE
Purpose of Checklist: 1-INIT   2-INIT COMPL   3-SPEC CORR   4-SUB   5-REINIT 6-CHECK REV

___

CURRENT PERIOD	SALES TAX
Price _ _ _ _ _ _ . _ _ _	Included: YES NO
Type of Price: REG SALE	

YEAR-ROUND in-season: JAN FEB MAR APR MAY JUN JUL AUG SEP OCT NOV DEC

Respondent: Location:

Field Message:

CLUSTER 02 - COMPONENTS AND OTHER SOUND EQUIPMENT

TYPE
  A1 Individual component
  A2 Component system put together by outlet or consumer
  A3 Component system put together by manufacturer
  A4 Compact systems
  A5 Convertible home/portable component system

COMPONENT(S) SELECTED FOR PRICING (Reporting of a price is optional)

  B1 Receiver   ** C99 $_____

  D1 Turntable   ** E99 $_____

  F1 Compact disk player (CD)   ** G99 $_____

  H1 Tape deck   ** I99 $_____

J1 Tuner   ** K99 $_____

L1 Integrated amplifier   ** M99 $_____

N1 Preamplifier   ** P99 $_____

Q1 Power amplifier   ** R99 $_____

S99 Speaker(s), Number   ** T99 $_____

_____ U1 Casceiver   ** V99
$_____ W1 Equalizer   ** X99
$_____
    Y1 Headphones   ** AA99 $_____

AB1 Phono cartridge (only   ** AC99 $_____
      priced with turntable)
AD99 Other component,   ** AE99 $_____

_____
AF99 Other component,   ** AG99 $_____

_____

AH1 Audio component rack   ** AI99 $_____

AJ99 Other equipment,   ** AK99 $_____

_____
AL99 Other equipment,   ** AM99 $_____

_____
AN99 Other equipment,   ** AP99 $_____

_____

BRAND, LINE AND MODEL NUMBER OF A3 OR A5

AX99 _____

BRAND AND MODEL NUMBER OF COMPACT SYSTEM - A4

AY99 _____

Casceiver - Use the specifications for receivers and tape decks for reporting

Compact system - Use the specifications for receivers, turntables, speakers and
  if applicable tape decks for reporting.

RECEIVER   TURNTABLE

BRAND   BRAND

 BA99 _____   CA99 _____

MODEL NUMBER   MODEL NUMBER

 BB99 _____   CB99 _____

RECEIVING CAPABILITIES   CAPABILITIES
  BC1 FM stereo   CC1 Single play (only one record)

47

BD1 AM stereo
BD2 AM monaural
BE99 Other bands _____WATTAGE
OPTIONAL PHONO CARTRIDGE
BG99 _____/Channel

REMOTE CONTROL
BH1 Not available
BH2 Standard
BH3 Optional and not included
BH4 Optional and included

CC2 Multiplay changer

CD1 Cartridge not included
CD2 Cartridge included by dealer
CD3 Cartridge included by manufacturer

BRAND AND MODEL OF PHONO CARTRIDGE
CE99 _____

REMOTE CONTROL
CF1 Not available
CF2 Standard
CF3 Optional and not included
CF4 Optional and included

COMPACT DISC PLAYER

BRAND

CH99 _____

MODEL NUMBER
CI99 _____

CAPABILITIES
CJ99 Multidisc changer, # of disc

_____

DC99 _____
CK1 Three Beam
CK2 One beam
CK99 Other _____

PROGRAMMABILITY
CL99 Random access programmability,
       number of tracks programmable

_____

CM99 Continuous playback of selected track,
       number of times

_____

CN1 Continuous playback of entire disc

FEATURES
CP1 Music scan
CQ99 Other _____

CR99 Other _____

CS99 Other _____

TAPE DECK

TYPE
DA1 Cassette (compact cassette)
DA2 DAT (Digital Audio Tape)
DA3 Reel-to-reel
DA99 Other

_____

BRAND CJ1 Single disc
DB99 _____

MODEL NUMBERTYPE OF LASER PICK-UP

NOISE REDUCTION SYSTEM
DG1 Dolby B
DH1 Dolby C system
                          DI1 DBX II system
DJ99 Other, system

CAPABILITIES
DK1 Single cassette
DK2 Dual cassette

REMOTE CONTROL
DL1 Remote control not available
DL2 Remote control standard
DL3 Remote control optional
      and not included
DL4 Remote control optional
      and included

INTEGRATED AMPLIFIER

BRAND
FA99 _____

MODEL NUMBER

REMOTE CONTROL   FB99 _____ CT1

Not available

  CT2 Standard   WATTAGE

  CT3 Optional and not included   FC99 _____ RMS/Channel CT4

Optional and included

                                 REMOTE CONTROL --------------------------------------

-----------------------   FD1 Remote control not available

TUNER   FD2 Remote control standard

                                FD3 Remote control optional and not included

BRAND   FD4 Remote control optional and included

  EA99 _____

MODEL NUMBER

  EB99 _____

  RECEIVING CAPABILITIES

    EC1 FM stereo

    ED1 AM stereo

    ED2 AM monaural

    EE99 Other, Bands

    _____

  REMOTE CONTROL

    EF1 Not available

    EF2 Standard

    EF3 Optional and not included

    EF4 Optional and included

PREAMPLIFIER   EQUALIZER

BRAND   BRAND

  GA99 _____   JA99 _____

MODEL NUMBER   MODEL NUMBER

  GB99 _____   JB99 _____

REMOTE CONTROL   TYPE

  GC1 Remote control not available   JC1 Graphic

  GC2 Remote control standard   JC2 Parametric

  GC3 Remote control optional   JC99 Other _____

      and not included GC4 Remote control optional   NUMBER OF

BANDS   and included   JD98

  _____   JD99 _____-----

POWER AMPLIFIER   HEADPHONESBRAND

                 BRAND   HA99 _____

  JG99 _____

MODEL NUMBER   MODEL NUMBER   HB99

  _____   JH99 _____

AMPLIFICATION
    HC1 Stereo only
    HC2 Stereo and monaural
    HC3 Monaural only
    HC99 Other _____

WATTAGE
　HE99 _____ RMS/Channel

SPEAKERS
　BRAND
　IA99 _____

　MODEL NUMBER
　IB99 _____

REPRODUCTION　IC1　Two way sound
CONSTRUCTION MATERIAL　IC2　Three way sound
Wood　IC99　Other _____

　WOOFER SIZE (if stated)
　　ID1　6 inch
　　IE1　8 inch
　　IF1　10 inch
　　IG1　12 inch
　　IH99　Other,

AUDIO COMPONENT RACK

BRAND
　KA99 _____
MODEL NUMBER
　KB99 _____
SIZE
　KC99　Width _____

　KD99　Height _____

　KE99　Depth _____
　　　　　　　　　　　　　　MAIN
　　　　　　　　　　　　　　　　　　　　KF1
　　　KF2　Metal
　KF99　Other _____
　KG1　Without doors
　KG2　With doors
　KH99　Door material

OTHER COMPONENTS AND/OR EQUIPMENT _____ TYPE　LA99
_____
BRAND　LB99 _____
MODEL NUMBER
　LC99 _____

OTHER COMPONENTS AND/OR EQUIPMENT
_____

TYPE　MA99 _____ BRAND　MB99
_____

MODEL NUMBER
　MC99 _____

The following section may be completed for any item priced.

** ADDITIONAL AND CLARIFYING DATA

　NA99 _____

　NB99 _____

　NC99 _____

www.ingramcontent.com/pod-product-compliance
Lightning Source LLC
Chambersburg PA
CBHW080912290526
45795CB00007BA/2507